Addresses on
THE EPISTLES OF JOHN
and an Exposition of
THE EPISTLE OF JUDE

Addresses on
THE EPISTLES OF JOHN

and an Exposition of

THE EPISTLE OF JUDE

by

H. A. IRONSIDE, Litt. D.

*author of Notes and Addresses covering
the entire New Testament.*

LOIZEAUX BROTHERS
Neptune, New Jersey

FIRST EDITION, NOVEMBER 1931
SECOND EDITION, JUNE 1949
NINETEENTH PRINTING, SEPTEMBER 1983

ISBN 0-87213-372-9

PREFACE

These addresses are published, with some revision and curtailment, practically as given during the winter and spring of 1930 and 1931, when it was my privilege to minister the Word in the D. L. Moody Memorial Church in Chicago, Illinois. The reader will find no attempts at elaborate or scholarly exegesis, but plain practical expositions of these letters of the Apostle John.

The fact that they were given **to** constantly changing audiences as well as to the regular attendants, accounts for the occasional necessity of repetition. Some reiterations have been eliminated, but where it seemed necessary for continuity of thought, others have been allowed to stand. The addresses are published in this permanent form in accord with the earnest solicitation of many who heard them and who felt that in this way they might be blessed to others who had not been present when they were delivered. If this result shall follow I shall unfeignedly thank God.

—H. A. IRONSIDE.

Chicago, Illinois,
June, 1931.

CONTENTS

CONTENTS

The First Epistle of John

The Reality of Christ's Manhood

"That which was from the beginning, which we have heard, which we have seen with our eyes, which we have looked upon, and our hands have handled, of the Word of life; (for the life was manifested, and we have seen it, and bear witness, and show unto you that eternal life, which was with the Father, and was manifested unto us); that which we have seen and heard declare we unto you, that ye also may have fellowship with us: and truly our fellowship is with the Father, and with His Son Jesus Christ. And these things write we unto you, that your joy may be full" (I John 1: 1-4).

The writings of the Apostle John have always had a peculiar charm for the people of the Lord, and I suppose, if for no other reason, for this, that they are particularly addressed to the family of God as such.

If you want truth concerning the kingdom of God in its present aspect, during the mystery days of the kingdom, you will find it in the epistles of Peter, James, and Jude. If you desire truth concerning the Church of God, the Body of Christ, which is being formed by the Spirit during the present dispensation of grace, you find that in the writings of the Apostle Paul. But if you seek truth for the family of God—the believer looked upon as one born again into the divine family— you find that particularly in the writings of the Apostle John. I do not mean, however, that any of these sections of Scripture are confined to the subjects indicated, for while Peter treats primarily of the kingdom, he also speaks of the Church and of the family of God; while Paul treats primarily of the Church, he also speaks of the kingdom and of the family, and while John treats primarily of the family, he also has something to say about the Church and about the kingdom. But God gave a special ministry to each of these New Testament writers, as indicated.

John's writings were the latest given by the Spirit of God for our edification. There are some dear people who put, it seems to me, undue value upon the writings of Paul, particularly his later ones, those which they call his "prison epistles," as though these contain the last instruction that God had for His people. However, Paul had been in heaven for probably over twenty years before the Apostle John wrote his Gospel. Then it was years later that John wrote his epistles, and the book of Revelation was, so far as we can learn, the last book given by the Spirit, almost at the end of the first century of the Christian era; so we may be sure of this much—that as God reserved the writings of the Apostle John for the close of the apostolic age, He kept the best wine until the last.

In the Gospel of John we have eternal life as manifested in the Son of God, our Lord Jesus Christ. In the epistles of John we have eternal life as manifested now in the children of God, those who through grace have been born into His family. In the last verse of the twentieth chapter of the Gospel the apostle gives his reason for writing that particular book. He says, "Many other signs truly did Jesus in the presence of His disciples, which are not written in this book; but these are written, that ye might believe that Jesus is the Christ, the Son of God; and that, believing, ye might have life through His name." Why was the Gospel of John written? In order that we might believe that Jesus is the Christ. Is there any one here who has any doubt of that, who finds himself questioning whether Jesus is in very truth the Christ of God? Read the Gospel of John. "Faith cometh by hearing, and hearing by the word of God" (Rom. 10: 17). And this particular portion of Holy Scripture was written that you might know, that you might "believe that Jesus is the Christ, the Son of God; and that believing ye might have life through His name."

Now look at the thirteenth verse of the fifth chapter of the first epistle of John, "These things have I written unto you that believe on the name of the Son of God; that ye may know that ye have eternal life, and that ye may believe on the name of the Son of God."

The Gospel was written that you might "believe that Jesus is the Christ . . . and that believing you might have life through His name." The epistle is written to people who already believe that Jesus is the Christ, but have never been settled on the question of their present position or of the possession of eternal life. "That ye might *know*." If you have any doubt as to the personality of Jesus, if you have any doubt as to the life and atoning death of Jesus, as to His Messiahship, or as to His Divinity, read the Gospel. But now, if having believed the message of the Gospel, you are still in perplexity as to the question of assurance, whether you really possess eternal life or not, read the epistle; for it is written to "you that believe on the name of the Son of God; that ye may know that ye have eternal life." The epistle of John is the epistle of fellowship; it shows us the way into fellowship with God, for He wants His people to be in communion with Him.

John uses certain key words or phrases: "Ye know," or "we know." He would have us rest on nothing short of definite, positive knowledge of a divine reality. Then there is the word "believe." That is one of his favorite words, both in the Gospel and in the epistles. We also read a great deal about "light"—*"God is light," "Walk in light."* Then there is the word "love"—*"God is love."* We are to *"walk in love."*

After the death of Paul, somewhere around A. D. 67, there arose among the churches, particularly in Asia, a sect that we know today as Gnostics. An agnostic, you know, is a man who says, "I do not know." People seem to like that term; some of our young folk go off to college and when they get a smattering of knowledge, they say, "I am an agnostic; I don't believe in this and I don't believe in that." Charles Spurgeon used to say that *agnostic* is but the Greek word for the Latin *ignoramus*. So that one might say, "I don't believe the Bible, because I am an ignoramus!" However, as a rule the agnostic likes his Greek name better than his Latin one. But a gnostic is the very opposite to an agnostic. The agnostic says, "I do not know;" the gnostic says, "I do know."

There came into the Church those who said, "We have superior knowledge to that of these simple Christians;" and this sect grew very rapidly, and threatened for two hundred years to overwhelm the orthodox portion of the Church of God. They had peculiar ideas in regard to Jesus. Some of them thought that Jesus was simply a man, the natural-born son of Joseph and Mary, and that the Christ was the Divine Spirit who came and took possession of Jesus at His baptism in Jordan and was with Him through life, but left Him when He hung on the cross. These were called Cerin-

thian gnostics. Today there are those who tell
you the same thing, that Jesus was a man and
Christ was a Spirit who took possession of Him.
This is the basic doctrine in Christian Science,
New Thought, The Unity School of Christianity,
and in Theosophy, and other modern cults. But
this is thoroughly contrary to Scripture, for it
says, "Every spirit that confesseth that Jesus is
the Christ is of God"—not that Jesus was possessed by the Christ or was controlled by the
Christ, but He is the Christ, and the One who
hung on the cross was not only Jesus, the man of
Nazareth, but, we read, *"Christ* died for our sins."
So we must never distinguish in that way between
Jesus and the Christ any more than we would distinguish between Mr. Hoover and the President.
Mr. Hoover *is* the President, and Jesus *is* the
Christ. It is perfectly true that Christ is a title,
but that title belongs to Him.

There was another set of gnostics, the
Doketists, who denied the reality of the manhood
of our Lord Jesus Christ—the reality of His human body. They held that all evil was linked with
the flesh, and therefore it was unthinkable that
Deity should ever condescend to dwell in a tabernacle of clay. If, for instance, while you gazed
upon Him you had attempted to take hold of Him,
you would have laid hold of thin air, He was
simply a phantom. John meets both these systems in his three epistles.

The opening verses of this chapter deal particularly with the Doketic system. Listen to John, "That which was from the beginning, which we have heard, which we have seen with our eyes, which we have looked upon, and our hands have handled, of the Word of life. For the life was manifested, and we have seen it, and bear witness, and show unto you that eternal life, which was with the Father, and was manifested unto us." What does John mean? Why, this eternal life has been manifested on earth in a Man. We heard that Man speak; we listened to His words, looked upon His face; we handled Him, we know that He was a real Man; we walked with Him for three and one-half wonderful years. And now John is saying, If you want the truth as to Christ, do not take up with these things that spring up overnight like mushrooms, but go back to that which was from the beginning. For of this we may be sure, "What is new is not true, and what is true is not new."

There are three distinct beginnings emphasized in Scripture. We read, "In the beginning God created the heaven and the earth" (Gen. 1: 1). That was the beginning of creation. Some imagine that was about 6,000 years ago; it might have been much more than that, but the Bible does not say. But go back as far as you will and you still find that, "In the beginning God created the heaven and the earth." Whenever that event took place, it was God who did it; He was there; He brought the universe into existence. It may have gone through a great many changes before the conditions described in the second verse of Genesis 1, but it was created by a personal God in the beginning, the beginning of creation. Then in John 1: 1 we read, "In the beginning was the Word, and the Word was with God, and the Word was God." That is the unbeginning beginning. When everything that ever had beginning began, the Word *was*. He had no beginning but was the eternally existing Son subsisting in the bosom of the Father. Then in the first chapter of this epistle, "That which was from the beginning" is not the beginning of the creation, neither is it the unbeginning beginning of John 1, but it is the beginning of the new dispensation; the beginning of Christianity when the truth was revealed in Christ.

Look at several scriptures that bring this out. I John 2: 7: "Brethren, I write no new commandment unto you, but an old commandment, which ye had *from the beginning.* The old commandment is the word which ye have heard *from the beginning.*" This refers to the teaching of our Lord Jesus Christ, the commandment given by Him. When was that given? From the beginning of Christianity, from the beginning of the new dispensation. The old commandment is the word which ye have heard from the beginning.

In other words, John is saying, "Do not take up with anything new; go back to that which was from the beginning of Christianity." Then read verse 14, "I have written unto you, fathers, because ye have known Him [that is] from the beginning."* He is here writing to the "fathers" who have known Him from the beginning of this new age of grace. Then in verse 24 we read, "Let that therefore abide in you, which ye have heard from the beginning. If that which ye have heard from the beginning shall remain in you, ye also shall continue in the Son, and in the Father." In 2 John 5 we find these words, "And now I beseech thee, lady, not as though I wrote a new commandment unto thee, but that which we had from the beginning, that we love one another." Don't go in for something new. That message which you received at the beginning is the message to which you must cling and is that which must abide in you. These passages make it clear that this term "from the beginning" does not, as some have thought, refer to eternity. It is from the start of the new era.

When people come to you and say, "We have a new doctrine, a new teaching, a new system of things," you can say, "Keep it; as for me I will cling firmly to that which was from the begin-

---

* There is nothing in the original answering to the italicized words of the A. V. "that is."

ning." We have a "faith which was once delivered unto the saints" (Jude 3).

The Mormon says, "We believe the Bible, but
we have the Mormon Bible too, and it is a new
revelation," but you reply, "I do not need your
new book. I have that which was from the beginning." When Mrs. Mary Baker Patterson
Glover Eddy says, "Of course we believe the Bible,
but here is my little book, 'Science and Health,'
which is something new," you say, "Thank you,
madam; I do not need your Key to the Scriptures;
the Word of God interpreted by the Holy Spirit
is all I need." When the Swedenborgians say,
"Surely we believe the Bible, but we add to it the
dreams and visions of Emanuel Swedenborg," we
reply in the words of Scripture, "He that hath a
dream let him tell a dream; and he that hath
My word, let him speak My word faithfully"
(Jer. 23: 28). When Pastor Russell and Judge
Rutherford come along and say, "Of course we
believe the Bible, but we must add to it our
'Studies in the Scriptures' and 'the Harp of God,'
if you would really understand it," we say, "Keep
all your seven or ten volumes; we will go back to
that which we have heard from the beginning. We
do not want anything added to the Scripture; we
go back to that which God gave at the first."

John shows that Jesus was a real Man, for he
declares, "We have heard Him; we listened to His
teaching as we walked with Him; we heard Him

speak; we have seen Him with our eyes." The gnostics said that He was merely a phantasm, but John insists on His true humanity, "That which we have *looked on intently.*" He was not deceived. Somebody comes up to me and says, "I want you to meet my friend, Mrs. So-and-so;" I say, "I am glad to meet you," and I turn away because others are crowding about me. The next day I meet this person on the street and she says, "Don't you know me?" I reply, "Your face is familiar; where did I meet you?" "Why, I met you yesterday at the Moody Church." I have to say, "I beg your pardon; the trouble is I did not gaze intently enough to have your features impressed upon me." The apostle says, "We were not deceived; we saw Him and gazed intently upon Him; we know He was a real Man, and He filled the vision of our souls." Then he adds, "That which our hands have handled, of the Word of life." It was not merely that he heard and looked, but he laid hold upon Him, and when he laid hold upon His arm, it was not thin air; and when John lay upon His breast at supper, it was not a delusion. Christ Jesus is a Man of true flesh and blood!

What a wonderful thing it is that the very first truth in the Christian revelation is that God became Man—the amazing grace of it all; God came down into His own world as a Man, came so near to us in order that He might reveal Himself to us and die for our sins. He was made a little

lower than the angels in order that He might
settle the sin question for us, and so the apostle
says in verse 2, which is really parenthetical, "For
the life was manifested, and we have seen it, and
bear witness, and show unto you that eternal life,
which was with the Father, and was manifested
unto us." Think of it! Eternal life was manifested on earth!

Do you want to know what eternal life really
is in all its fulness, in all its purity? Study the
life of Jesus; read the four Gospels. John says,
"The Word was made flesh, and *tabernacled*
among us, and we beheld His glory, the glory as
of the only begotten of the Father, full of grace
and truth" (John 1: 14). Although you and I do
not see Him now with our natural eyes, yet
through the testimony of John and his fellow-
apostles we are enabled to see Jesus, to see the
manifestation of eternal life. So he says, in verse
3, "That which we have seen and heard declare
we unto you, that ye also may have fellowship
with us: and truly our fellowship is with the
Father, and with His Son Jesus Christ."

Fellowship is a distinctly New Testament word.
I do not mean that you will not find the English
word in our translation of the Old Testament, but
there it has the thought of *companionship*. In
Christianity it is far more. When you hear the
benediction pronounced, "The love of God and the
communion of the Holy Spirit, and the grace of

our Lord Jesus Christ be with you," do you stop and think of what that means? People of altogether different heredity, different environment, different cultural standards, saved by the same grace, indwelt by the same Holy Spirit, are brought into marvelous fellowship one with another.

I remember a number of years ago sitting at a table eating with two Christian workers, one a colored man, the other a Japanese. Suddenly my Japanese friend said to us in his quiet oriental way, "What a wonderful thing is the grace of God! Just look at this, a black man, a yellow man, and a white man, all one in Christ Jesus! By nature each one filled with suspicion of the other, and even with a feeling of repugnance toward each other, but by grace all one in Christ." This is not something artificially pumped up or produced by any effort of your own, but it is the effect of the indwelling Holy Spirit of God, the work of the third Person of the Trinity.

But now the object of fellowship is occupation with Christ. We read, "Truly our fellowship is with the Father and with His Son Jesus Christ." In 1 Corinthians 1: 9 we read, "God is faithful, by whom ye have been called into the fellowship of His Son." Men try to get up fellowships, and they are poor things at the best. The only fellowship I know anything about is the fellowship of God's dear Son. Men may have these fellowships if they will, but, thank God, every believer has been called into the fellowship of God's Son. The Apostle John says, "Our fellowship is with the Father and with His Son Jesus Christ." I like that—*our fellowship.*

I remember years ago I was telling a brother about a certain missionary, and this brother to whom I was speaking happened to be one of a particular group of Christians with which I am intimately associated. He looked rather bored while I was speaking with him, and when I had finished he said, "And is the brother in our fellowship?" "If you mean some little clique of Christians, no, I do not think he is in our fellowship; but if you mean the fellowship of the Son of God, yes, he is in our fellowship." Our fellowship is the fellowship of the Body of Christ as set forth in the communion, "The bread which we break, is it not the communion of the Body of Christ?" What a marvelous fellowship this is!

Do you want to know how to get into this fellowship? There is only one way—through a second birth and the gift of the Holy Spirit of God. Believe in the Lord Jesus Christ, be born again, and the Spirit will come to dwell in you and bring you into "our fellowship." Fellowship means common thoughts and interests. Have you learned to know a Saviour's love? Do you enjoy the precious things that the Apostle John is telling us about? Has the glorious truth of eternal life as revealed in the Son of God become a reality to you? Then let us share it together. I know a little about Christ and you tell me a little of that which you know, and our hearts are warmed. That is real fellowship.

John concludes this section with these words, "And these things write we unto you, that your joy may be full." You have a measure of joy now; you will have more as you get better acquainted with Christ. You have a measure of happiness now; you will have more as you get to know Him more intimately.

The fifth verse begins the message that John gives to Christians in order to bring them into the fulness of that fellowship with God.

The Christian Message

"This then is the message which we have heard of Him, and declare unto you, that God is light, and in Him is no darkness at all. If we say that we have fellowship with Him, and walk in darkness, we lie, and do not the truth: but if we walk in the light, as He is in the light, we have fellowship one with another, and the blood of Jesus Christ His Son cleanseth us from all sin. If we say that we have no sin, we deceive ourselves, and the truth is not in us. If we confess our sins, He is faithful and just to forgive us our sins, and to cleanse us from all unrighteousness. If we say that we have not sinned, we make Him a liar, and His word is not in us. My little children, these things write I unto you, that ye sin not. And if any man sin, we have an Advocate with the Father, Jesus Christ the righteous: and He is the propitiation for our sins: and not for our's only, but also for the sins of the whole world" (1 John 1: 5 to 2: 2).

In this section John gives us in brief the Christian message—a synopsis of that evangel which the Lord Jesus Christ commissioned His apostles to carry into all the world, which if believed fills the heart with joy. What is the message? "This then is the message which we have heard of Him, and declare unto you, that God is light, and in Him is no darkness at all." They had heard it from His own lips while He was on earth. You may say, "I do not see anything about this that is particularly cheering, especially heartening, anything that would fill my soul with joy." If you are going on to know fulness of joy, you must begin with this; the soul must first of all be brought into the presence of God as He is; and God is light.

There are two expressions used in this book that tell us the nature of God. Here we read that God is *light,* and in chapter 4 we read that God is *love.* Now God is gracious, but you could not say that God is grace. God is merciful, but you could not say that God is mercy. But we can say that God is loving and that He is love. And so, in the same way, the apostle says, "God is light." This is His very nature. What does this mean?

Light is used throughout Scripture as a synonym for infinite holiness, purity, perfect righteousness. "God is light, and in Him is no darkness at all." There is nothing in God but absolute purity, absolute perfection, absolute holiness. You say, "Well, how then can I, a guilty sinner, ever have fellowship with that infinitely holy God? I might as well give up at once, for if 'God is light, and in Him is no darkness at all,' if He can discern every secret thought of my heart, if He sees every evil way in me, how can I ever have fellowship with Him?" He has provided the way, but He first would have me recognize this, that if I ever have fellowship with Him, it must be *in the light,* and so John goes on to say, "If we say that we have fellowship with Him, and walk in

darkness, we lie, and do not the truth." There is
no use talking about having fellowship with God
and living in sin. "He that covereth his sins shall
not prosper: but whoso confesseth and forsaketh
them shall have mercy" (Prov. 28: 13). To walk
in darkness is to walk in sin; to walk in sin is
to follow the dictates of our own natural minds
and hearts. "For ye were sometimes darkness,
but now are ye light in the Lord: walk as children
of light" (Eph. 5: 8). "Having the understanding darkened, being alienated from the life of
God through the ignorance that is in them, because of the blindness of their heart" (Eph. 4:
18). This is the description of all men by nature; the unsaved man belongs to the darkness;
he is in Satan's kingdom of darkness, and walks
in it and loves it. Scripture says, "Men loved
darkness rather than light, because their deeds
were evil." If you are doing something shameful,
something corrupt, something vile, you do not
want to do it in the full blaze of the light of day;
you seek some hidden place either alone or with
some companion like yourself. You cannot have
fellowship with God in darkness, for God is light.

We have darkness presented in four different
ways in Scripture. There is the natural darkness,
"having the understanding darkened"—this is
true of all men by nature. No man by nature un-
derstands God. No man naturally loves holiness
and purity. Have you ever noticed that you do not

have to teach little children to tell lies, but you do have to teach them to tell the truth; you never have to teach them to lose their temper, but you have to teach them to control it; you never have to teach them to be disobedient, but you do have to teach them to be obedient? Why is this? Because men naturally are children of darkness. As we look into the faces of babes we do not like to think that in their little hearts there is the same sinful tendency that we find in ourselves, but it is there nevertheless, and therefore there is the necessity of regeneration: "Ye must be born again."

Men say, "I am not responsible, because I was born a sinner, because my understanding was darkened; God is responsible for permitting me to come into the world like this." God accepts full responsibility, and is not going to send any one to eternal judgment because he was born a sinner; He is not going to send any one to everlasting ruin because he was born in darkness; but the blessed God has come to men and offered them a way out, and that way we find in the gospel.

In the second place, we have wilful darkness, and our Lord Jesus says, "This is the condemnation (not that men were born sinners), that light is come into the world, and men loved darkness rather than light, because their deeds were evil." "He that doeth truth cometh to the light, that his deeds may be made manifest, that they are wrought in God" (John 3: 21), but every one that does evil hates the light.   Men are therefore responsible when they reject the light that comes to them.   That is the condemnation; that is wilful darkness.

We know that the solemn result of this is judicial darkness.   In Jeremiah 13: 16 we read, "Give glory to the Lord your God, before He cause darkness, and before your feet stumble upon the dark mountains, and, while ye look for light, He turn it into the shadow of death, and make it gross darkness."   You may say, "Does this God who is light sometimes cause darkness?"   Yes, if men deliberately reject the light, if men deliberately turn their backs upon the light.   Pharaoh did this; he hardened himself against God, and God then hardened him in his sins.   In 2 Thessalonians 2 we read of those who "received not the love of the truth, that they might be saved. And for this cause God shall send them strong delusion, that they should believe a lie: that they all might be damned who believed not the truth but had pleasure in unrighteousness."   My friend, if God has given you a measure of light, thank Him for it, and seek grace to go on in that light and not to turn away from it, lest you go into judicial darkness.

In Jude we read of the final result of rejecting the light—"To whom is reserved the blackness of darkness for ever" (Jude 13). If you are given to Universalism and like to believe the dream of the final restoration of all men to God, see what you can make out of that verse. There are certain men for whom is "reserved the blackness of darkness for ever." But God does not want any man to live in the dark or die in the dark; He wants men to come into the light, and in order that they may do so He has come to them. The veil that once separated between God and man was rent asunder, from top to bottom, when Christ died, and now the true light is shining, and, "If we walk in the light, as He is in the light, we have fellowship one with another, and the blood of Jesus Christ His Son cleanseth us from all sin."

Of old God dwelt in the thick darkness. Man sought in vain to find out or comprehend Him. But now God is "in the light;" He has been fully manifested. He is no longer hidden. He has been perfectly revealed in Christ; and the rent vail permits His glory to shine forth.

Notice that the cleansing of the blood depends upon our walking in the light. What is it then that the apostle is telling us? I remember for years I was in a great deal of confusion of mind about this. I read it as though it said, "If we walk *according to* the light, the blood of Jesus Christ His Son cleanseth us from all sin." I thought it meant that if I was very punctilious about obeying every command of God, that if I walked according to all the light I might have, He would cleanse me, which was really only saying that I was cleansed when I did not need cleansing.

We find that the vilest sinner may have this cleansing. When does he get it? Why, when he turns away from the darkness and comes to the light. Notice, it does not say if we walk *according* to light, but it says, "If we walk *in* the light." It is *where* you walk, not *how* you walk. It is to walk in the presence of God. By nature we do not want to come into the presence of God, but when the Holy Spirit has done His convicting work in our souls, we cannot stay away any longer, and we run toward the light, making our way into the very presence of the One we have been dreading, and we find the light is shining from the blood-sprinkled mercy-seat.

You remember the picture in the Tabernacle. In the holiest of all there was the ark of the covenant, the mercy-seat, and the cherubim overshadowing it. They are indicated in the Psalms as setting forth divine justice and judgment. As a poor sinner, justice and judgment are waiting, as it were, to visit divine wrath upon my guilty soul, but here the divine justice and judgment are seen above the mercy-seat. What is it that constitutes the throne of God a mercy-seat? It is sprinkled with blood, the blood of sacrifice, and so the divine justice and judgment are gazing down upon the blood, and it is in the very place from which the light shines. Between the cherubim is an uncreated light, the Shekinah glory. I who at one time shrank from the light, loving my sin and the darkness, now led on by the Spirit of God, come to the light, face it, and let it shine full upon me, and what does it manifest? It manifests my sin and my iniquity. But I am not alone there, for, "If we walk in the light, as He is in the light, we have fellowship one with another." I find that I am simply one of a great group of people who are all just as bad as I am by nature. Many people have an idea that they never could be happy coming into the presence of God until they first become saints, but the first time you come into His presence, you must come with all your sins upon you, either in this life or in the day of judgment. If you come into His presence with your sins upon you in the day of judgment, it will mean that you will be lost forever; but if in this life, then you will find that though the light shows up all the corruption and iniquity and wickedness, the blood is in the very place from which the light comes. "The blood of Jesus Christ His Son cleanseth us from all sin." Again I say, It is not *how* we walk, it is *where* we walk. Do you walk in the light; have you come into the presence of God; have you ever had that light shine upon you?

The word *cleanseth* suggests to many a continual cleansing, but I do not think that is the thought

of Scripture. The marvelous thing is that when
you put your trust in the Lord Jesus, the blood
of Christ cleanses eternally and completely in the
sight of God. Here is the blessed fact: the blood
abides upon the mercy-seat; it is there constantly
before God in its eternal efficacy. There is never
a moment that the blood is not there before God.
I may be conscious of failure in words, deeds,
and thoughts that grieve the Spirit of God, but
the blood abides and it cleanseth from all sin.

When it comes to practical cleansing we have
the washing of water by the Word. God's esti-
mate of the sacrificial work of His Son will never
change, and therefore my standing before God will
never change.

> "Once in Him, in Him forever,
>   Thus God's faithful record stands."

When it says, "The blood of Jesus Christ His
Son cleanseth us from *all* sin," it might be translated, "The blood of Jesus Christ His Son cleanseth us from *every* sin." It cleanses from the guilt
of sin. The moment I put my trust in the Lord
Jesus Christ, the blood cleanses from it all. There
was a time when I thought of this as a kind of
inward experience. I thought of myself as a
Christian but with a sinful nature, and that little
by little it would be cleansed; but the marvelous
fact is that over against all my guilt is the infinite value of the atoning blood of the Lord Jesus

Christ. God does not see one sin resting upon the soul that trusts that precious blood.

Now, "If we say we have no sin, we deceive ourselves, and the truth is not in us." Suppose one says, "I have no need of this cleansing blood; I am good enough as I am; I am not a sinner; I am not a transgressor; I do not need forgiveness." One of our poets has said, "I need no Christ to die for me," and he is not the only one who takes that position to-day. Very well, the apostle says, "If we say we have no sin, we deceive ourselves." Mark, we do not deceive any one else; you never saw a man that could deceive his wife by saying he had no sin. He might have been able to deceive her before they were married, but she soon begins to see little flaws and cannot be deceived. We do not deceive those nearest and dearest; the only person that can be deceived is ourselves, and the Word goes on to tell us that "the truth is not in us."

I remember years ago when that princely man, Henry Varley, was having some meetings in Oakland, California, speaking on this verse he said, "I have been told that you have a good many sinless people out here in California. I have never seen one such person myself, and I have a real curiosity to see one; if there is one here to-night, I should like to see him as soon as the meeting is over." After the meeting, one man came up to the preacher and said. "I understand you want to

see a perfectly sinless man; I have never sinned
in twenty-two years, since I was wholly sanctified." "Well, now, my dear brother," said Mr.
Varley, "let me get this right. You recognize, of
course, that there are sins of omission as well as
of commission?" "Yes," he said. "And you are
telling me that you have never been guilty either
of sins of commission or of omission for twenty-
two years?" the preacher asked. The man started to justify himself when an old lady came up
the aisle, and before he could say a word, she said,
"Yes, there is some folks says they never commit
sins, but ask their neighbors, especially those who
keep chickens, what scratches up their lawns, and
they can tell a different story." The man left
without a word. "If we say we have no sin, we
deceive ourselves, and the truth is not in us."
That is why we need the cleansing value of the
precious blood of Christ.

As a believer in the Lord Jesus Christ, I can no
more stand before God on the ground of my own
spiritual experience than I could as a sinner. I
stand before Him on the ground of the redemption that is in Christ Jesus.

Can we go on then living in sin? No, not at all.
Cleansing by the blood is our judicial cleansing,
but what about the practical thing? "If we confess our sins, He is faithful and just to forgive
us our sins, and to cleanse us from all unrighteousness." This is our practical cleansing. You

see, I come to God not only wanting my sins put
away from before Him, my evil record expunged
from the books of eternity, but wanting practical
deliverance by His power, and also wanting to
know what it is to have actual cleansing in my
life in word and thought and deed. I must come
to God as a penitent, for it does not say that if
we pray our sins will be forgiven, but, "If we
confess our sins, He is faithful and just to forgive us our sins, and to cleanse us from all unrighteousness." Of course, as a sinner, when I
come to Christ I come on the ground of this verse,
and He cleanses me, but as a believer confessing
the failures in my life, I come confessing my sin,
and He is "faithful and just to forgive."

In the Old Testament men were to come to God
with an offering and confess that they had sinned
in *that thing*. This implies definiteness in confession. I am afraid many of us really never get to
God in confession because we are so indefinite.
Somebody prays and says, "If Thou hast seen any
sin, anything amiss in me, forgive me." Hold on
a minute! *Is* there anything amiss; do you know
of anything amiss? The proper way to make confession is to come to God acknowledging the wrong
I have done. A lady who came to Charles Wesley,
said, "I want you to pray with me; I am a great
sinner; I am a saint of God, but I do fail so dreadfully, and I want you to pray with me." Mr.
Wesley said rather sternly, "I will pray for you,

for indeed you need it; you are a great sinner."
"What do you mean?" she asked indignantly; "I
have never done anything very bad!" Oh, dear
friends, if you want blessing, do not confess your
sins in that way; get into the presence of God
and tell Him all about it, about that bad temper,
about that scandalous tongue, about all the things
that grieve His Holy Spirit. Some of you say,
"Pray for my husband, I would like him to be
converted." He is more likely to be converted if
you will say, "O God, I confess that my bad temper
is hindering my husband from being saved, it is
alienating my children; I am not surprised that
my friends are not converted." Then go to them
and make confession to them. If you have been
saying it was nervousness when it was really
bad temper, confess that it is temper, and stop
trying to excuse sin.

He will cleanse us by the washing of the Word,
and give victory in our lives, and enable us to
live here to His praise and glory. "If we say we
have not sinned (if we dare to take the ground
that we have never sinned) we make Him a liar,
and His word is not in us"—we have never yet
come into the light: we are still in the darkness
trying to cover up our sins. God give us to be real
with Him and with one another, and then we
shall know the blessing of fellowship in the light.

Christic our Advocate

"My little children, these things write I unto you, that ye sin not. And if any man sin, we have an Advocate with the Father, Jesus Christ the righteous: and He is the propitiation for our sins: and not for ours only, but also for the sins of the whole world" (1 John 2: 1, 2).

These two verses constitute the second part of the message which we were studying last Lord's Day. You remember in verse five of chapter one we read, "This then is the message," and then in the verses following, down through that chapter, including the two verses of the second chapter, we have the message in its entirety, the message which John and his fellow-apostles were commissioned by Christ to carry throughout the world. It is the message of man's utterly lost condition in the darkness, of the atoning value of the precious blood of Christ, of the importance of facing our sins in the presence of God, and when we thus face them we find forgiveness. And now John goes on to take up the question of the failures of believers, the ones who have been cleansed judicially from all sin. What about our failures?

—for you know we do fail, all of us, much as we may regret the sad fact.

I remember last summer I was rather amused listening to an address. The speaker was telling of a little girl who had been left by her parents with another family while they were away, and when at last the mother and father returned for her and she was on her way home, she said to her father:

"Daddy, there are four little boys at that house where I have been staying."

"Yes, I knew that," he said.

"Daddy, they have family worship there every night."

"I'm glad to hear that."

"Daddy, every night their father prays for those four little boys."

"That is very nice."

"He prays, Daddy, that God will make them good boys, and that they won't do anything naughty," said the little one.

"That is very nice."

She was silent a moment and then said, "But, Daddy, He hasn't done it yet."

There are a great many folk like that. We are praying that God will make us good, that God will make us holy, that our lives may be lives of victory, but I am afraid that many of us have to confess that "God hasn't done it yet." We recognize the fact that we do sin, that we do fail. Our hearts are nearly broken by our failures. What about the sins of believers?

In the first place, believers should not sin. John tells us, "My little children, these things write I unto you, that ye sin not. And if any man sin, we have an Advocate with the Father, Jesus Christ the righteous." The word translated *little children* might better be translated *children,* or *dear children,* because this original word has no reference whatever to age or size. It is a word that takes in all who are born of God. It literally means *born ones,* those who are born into God's family. "My children, these things write I unto you, that ye should not be sinning." It is then, the desire, the will of God for His children that we should not be sinning. God has redeemed us to Himself, not only to take us to heaven at last, but that we should live to the praise of His glory in this world.

A little farther on we read, "Whosoever is born of God doth not commit sin" (1 John 3:9), in the sense that they do not *live in the practice of sin.* When people are converted, a change takes place. If there is no change they have never been born of God. From that time they hate sin and love holiness; if they do not hate sin and love holiness, they are not born of God. On the other hand, I recognize the fact that "there is not a just man upon the earth, that doeth good, and sinneth not" (Eccl. 7:20), not one that does not fail. It is not that there is not power in God to deliver us, but there is not always in us the steadfastness to keep our eyes fixed on Christ, to reckon ourselves "to be dead indeed unto sin, but alive unto God through Jesus Christ our Lord."

The moment a believer becomes self-occupied, unwatchful, neglectful of prayer, you have sin. Let us remember that sin consists not merely in doing overt evil acts, but just as truly in not doing the good that you might. "To him that knoweth to do good, and doeth it not, to him it is sin" (James 4:17).

I frequently meet people who say they never sin. I ask them, "Just what do you mean by that? Do you mean that you never break any of the ten commandments?" "Yes," they say. "Do you mean that you never commit any actual overt acts of iniquity?" "Yes." "Do you also mean that you do everything that you know you could do for God, that you take advantage of every opportunity of doing good, of every opportunity of speaking for Christ, of every opportunity of in any way glorifying your Lord and Saviour?" If there is the least bit of honesty, they bow their head and say, "No, I am afraid that I do not." Then you sin, and sin is not merely the violation of certain moral principles, it is also failure to do the good that you might do.

"If any man sin"—here it is the Greek aorist— it means, "If any man commit a sin at a given point of time." It is not a question of the practice of sin, but of some definite failure. "If any man sin," what then? According to the thought that some have, if any man sin, that immediately severs the link that binds the believer to Christ. Oh, no. If that were true, not one of us would have the assurance that he was really a Christian for an hour at a time; but see, there are two links that bind us to Christ. First there is the link of union. That link is so strong that the weight of the world could not break it. Our blessed Lord Himself said, "My sheep hear My voice, and I know them, and they follow Me: and I give unto them eternal life: and they shall *never* perish" (John 10: 27, 28). Nothing can ever break that link when once it has been formed by the Spirit of God.

But there is another link that binds the believer to the Lord, and that is the link of communion. That is so delicate, is so easily broken, that one unholy thought will snap it, one unchristlike action will destroy it, one minute given to levity and foolishness will break it, and that link could never be formed again if it depended entirely upon us. We often speak of the finished work of Christ, and rightly so. Our blessed Lord as He hung upon that cross cried, "It is finished," and bowed His head and dismissed His spirit, and there the work that saves our guilty souls was completed. "Whatsoever God doeth, it shall be for ever; nothing can

be put to it, nor anything taken from it: and God
doeth it, that men should fear before Him" (Eccl.
3 : 14).   That finished work of Christ stands alone
in its absolute perfection, and on that finished
work we may well rest our souls.

A dear saint was dying, and somebody leaned
over him and said, "Do you feel that everything
is all right?"   He said, " 'It is finished;' upon that
I can rest my eternity."

> "Upon a life I did not live,
> Upon a death I did not die,
> Another's life, Another's death,
> I stake my whole eternity."

> "It is finished, yes, indeed;
> Finished, every jot!
> Sinner, this is all you need!
> Tell me, is it not?"

We cannot add anything to a finished work.

But while it is perfectly scriptural to speak of
the finished work of Christ, it is just as scriptural
to speak of the unfinished work of Christ, for our
blessed Lord who completed one work when He
died for our sins, began another when He ascended to the Father's right hand in heaven.   Up
there in the glory "He ever liveth to make intercession for us," and that work is looked at in two
aspects.   We read in Hebrews that He is there
as our High Priest with God.   As the High Priest
He is there to give us a perfect representation

before God. We are seen in Him, and He is there to minister grace in every time of need. As a High Priest, He who can be "touched with the feeling of our infirmities" sympathizes with us in all our weakness. His sympathy has nothing to do with our sins, it has to do with our infirmities, with our weaknesses. If we avail ourselves of His high priestly work, we will not fall into sin. We can go to Him, our great High Priest, and obtain mercy and find grace for every time of need.

Scripture not only presents Him thus, but also as our Advocate, and as such He has to do with the question of our sins as believers. He is said to be a High Priest with God, but He is our Advocate with the Father. The more I read this Book the more I realize the exactness of Scripture; the more I hear people talk about the Bible and the more I read it, the more I am impressed with how inexact we are when talking about divine things. It is quite natural for us to talk about the High Priest with the Father, or the Advocate with God, but that would dissipate the truth of Scripture. My sins are all put away by the blood of Christ, and I have a perfect representation before the throne of God in my great High Priest. "Wherefore He is able also to save them to the uttermost that come unto God by Him, seeing He ever liveth to make intercession for them" (Heb. 7: 25).

When I was converted, God became my Father. There is no such thing in the Bible as the universal Fatherhood of God, but He is the Father of those who are born again. As a believer if I fail, if I fall into sin, I read, "If any man sin, we have an Advocate with *the Father*." Not an Advocate with God merely, but with the Father. Why with the *Father?* Because the Spirit of God would teach me that relationship has not been disturbed! You remember that time you lost your temper and the devil said, "Now then you have done it; you were a Christian before, but not any more. God isn't your Father any more." That was simply one of the lies of the devil, for it is written, "If any man sin, we have an Advocate with *the Father*." Relationship was undisturbed. This word translated *Advocate* is exactly the same as the one used by our blessed Lord in John 14, 15, and 16, where He speaks of the *Comforter* that the Father will send in His name and whom He will send from the Father; for the Spirit of God is sent both by the Father and by the Son. In the original the word *Paraclete* means *one who comes to your side to help*. The Lord says, "I am going away, but I will send the Paraclete—One who will come to your side to help in every time of need."

On the other hand, "If any man sin, we have an Advocate—a Paraclete, a Helper—with the Father, Jesus Christ the righteous." In other words, God has sent the Holy Spirit down to earth to dwell in me, to be the Advocate here on earth to look after God's interests in me, and then too, the blessed Lord is up in the glory to be my Advocate with the Father, to look after my interests with the Father.

Why do I need an Advocate? Because I have a great adversary. An advocate is one who goes into court to represent you and to plead your case. You cannot do it yourself, but you go to your advocate, and he goes to plead your case against your adversary. So Satan is called in Revelation 12:10, the "accuser of our brethren, which accused them before our God day and night." The very moment we sin the devil constitutes himself the prosecuting attorney in the high court of heaven. You remember that time when you were guilty of that evil thing—you know the thing that you cannot forget—that moment the devil went right into the presence of God and said, "Is that one of your Christians? Listen to what he is saying now; see what he is doing—a Christian?" He is there to accuse, but the blessed Lord is there, and shows His wounds and spreads His hands, and says, "My Father, I took all that into account when I died on Calvary's tree."

> "I hear the accuser roar
>   Of ills that I have done;
> I know them well, and thousands more,
>   Jehovah findeth none."

"Though the restless foe accuses—
  Sins recounting like a flood,
  Ev'ry charge our God refuses;
  Christ has answered with His blood."

I realize my unrighteousness when I fall into
sin, and may well give up in despair, but I see I
have there in the presence of the Father the absolutely Righteous One to give me a perfect representation, and God sees me in Him. So I plead
not my own righteousness but that of God as
manifested in Christ Jesus, and you see I can
plead with power, I can plead with efficacy, because He has actually died for the very sin that
is now troubling me. "If any man sin, we have
an Advocate with the Father, Jesus Christ the
righteous: and He is the propitiation for our
sins."

This word, *propitiation,* as used in John's
epistle is a different word from that used in
Romans. The one in Romans means the *mercy-
seat.* When we there read, "Christ is the propitiation," it is the *mercy-seat,* the meeting-place
between God and man; but the word used here
and in the fourth chapter means an *atonement* or
an *expiation,* and my failures cannot undo the
work of the cross. Thank God, Christ has died
and has been raised, and has gone up to God's
right hand, and is there as my Advocate interced-
ing for me, and there He undertakes my case. He
Himself is the propitiation.

It does not say, "If any man repent, we have an Advocate; if any man confess his sins, we have an Advocate; if any man weep over his sins, we have an Advocate." What it does say is this, "If any man sin, we have an Advocate with the Father." It is not merely when I am penitent that I have an Advocate, but the very moment I fail Christ takes up my case, yes, even long before I have been exercised about it. The moment that hasty word left my lips, the moment I did that crooked thing, and did it thoughtlessly in some business matter perhaps, or something like that, that very moment before my conscience was exercised, before I was troubled, the devil was in the presence of God to accuse, but the same instant the Son of God was there to represent me, and as a result of His advocacy the Spirit takes the Word of God and applies it to my conscience, and then I begin to be exercised; I am troubled; I confess my sin. Possibly that exercise did not commence until some little time after my failure, perhaps I did not realize the true condition of things until that night I could not pray; I did not have liberty; and I said to myself, "What is the matter?" And then I cried, "Search me, O God, and know my heart; try me, and know my thoughts" (Ps. 139: 23). Now in answer to the advocacy of my blessed Lord the Spirit of God says, "Don't you remember that hasty word, that unholy thought, that crooked thing you did, that unforgiving spirit, that vanity, that carnality?" And it comes home to me, and I break before God and say, "O God, I cannot go to sleep tonight until I have told Thee all about it," and I tell my story, confess my failures, my weakness, my sins, and as I do so, I know the blessing of the Word, "If we confess our sins, He is faithful and just to forgive us our sins, and to cleanse us from all unrighteousness" (1 John 1: 9). You see the wonderful truth is that all the experiences I have gone through have not touched the question of my relationship in the family of God.

We have raised two boys, and sometimes those boys, for they are just like other boys, were mighty good, and sometimes they have given us a great deal of trouble. Sometimes they have given us a great deal of comfort, and then there have been other times when they have not been just all they ought to be, everything they should be, and it has troubled us a bit. We have had to discipline them and perhaps say to them, "You go up to your room and stay there until you can face this thing, until you are ready to acknowledge the wrong and ask forgiveness." Sometimes the child's will would set itself against the will of the parents, and hour after hour would go by and no acknowledgment would come, and then supper would be coming on and there would be the rattle of the dishes, and we would hear the call, "Father!" I would go upstairs and he would say,

"Am I not going down to supper?" "That depends on you; confess your wrong and you may come down." "Well," he would say, "if you think I have done anything wrong, I am sorry." "No, that won't do," and so I had to leave him and go down. Then I would begin to serve the meal and the odor would be wafted upstairs, and he would be getting hungry, and then another call, and again there would be a kind of shunning of the thing and he would say, "Since you and Mother both think it is wrong, I guess it is, and I am sorry." "No, guessing will not do," and I would have to turn again, and maybe half-way down the stairs I would hear the call, "Father, Father, please forgive me; I know I have done wrong; please forgive me; I have been awfully stubborn." Oh, how glad I was to throw my arms about him and put the kiss of forgiveness upon his forehead, and say, "Come on down; we will all enjoy dinner better with you there."

So it is with our God and Father. Sin does not touch the question of relationship, but it does touch communion, or fellowship; but our blessed Lord is in the presence of God the Father to plead for His people, and as a result of His advocacy we are brought to repent and confess, and He graciously restores our souls.

Obedience, the Proof of the New Life

"And hereby we do know that we know Him, if we keep His commandments. He that saith, I know Him, and keepeth not His commandments, is a liar, and the truth is not in him. But whoso keepeth His word, in him verily is the love of God perfected: hereby know we that we are in Him. He that saith he abideth in Him ought himself also so to walk, even as He walked. Brethren, I write no new commandment unto you, but an old commandment which ye had from the beginning. The old commandment is the word which ye have heard from the beginning. Again, a new commandment I write unto you, which thing is true in Him and in you: because the darkness is past, and the true light now shineth. He that saith he is in the light, and hateth his brother, is in darkness even until now. He that loveth his brother abideth in the light, and there is none occasion of stumbling in him. But he that hateth his brother is in darkness, and walketh in darkness, and knoweth not whither he goeth, because that darkness hath blinded his eyes" (1 John 2:3-11).

The apostle now brings before us some tests of Christian profession. It is one thing to say, "I am a Christian," but it is another thing to be the possessor of divine eternal life. It is one thing to say, "I am a child of God," and it is quite another to know the marvelous blessing of regeneration. Do we say we are Christians? Do we claim to be children of God? Then we must prove it by our lives.

"We do know that we know Him, if we keep

His commandments." He is not speaking from a legal standpoint; it is not, as of old, that the commandments of God are presented to us with a view of obtaining life. The law said of the man who keeps His commandments, "Which, if a man do, he shall live in them." But here, under grace, it is the opposite, the man who lives by faith will do His commandments. He who says he lives to God in Christ and yet is utterly indifferent to the will of God has never been born of God; he is still in "the gall of bitterness, and in the bond of iniquity" (Acts 8: 23). The child of God delights in obedience to the will of God; not, of course, that his obedience is perfect, for it is never that; there is only One who could say, "I do always those things that please Him" (John 8: 29). But where God has wrought the miracle of regeneration in the soul of a man, he finds within himself a love springing up for the will of God. He delights to walk in obedience to His Word, and thus he has corroborative evidence that he is a child of God. He not only rests upon the Word that says, "He that believeth on the Son hath everlasting life," but he finds within himself that which corroborates his faith, that which proves he has been born of God. This new desire to do the will of God is not of the natural man. By nature we prefer to do our own will, we prefer to take our own way; but trusting Christ, we learn to delight in the Divine will.

"He that saith, I know Him, and keepeth not His commandments, is a liar, and the truth is not in him." How outspoken the Apostle John is! Some folk do not appreciate strong language like this. But we need to realize that the apostle is dealing with certain great abstract truths; men either love God or do not, they either walk in darkness or they walk in light. There are no gradations in between. Great outstanding principles are here brought before us, and by these we may test ourselves and see where we are. We may ask, "Do I delight in the will of God; do I love His commandments?" If I do not, there is no use professing to be a Christian, for in doing so I am uttering a falsehood. It is hypocrisy to take the ground of being a believer while in works denying my profession.

"He that saith, I know Him, and keepeth not His commandments, is a liar, and the truth is not in him. But whoso keepeth His word, in him verily is the love of God perfected: hereby know we that we are in Him." There is a difference between keeping His word and keeping His commandments. Of course, a little farther down we are told that "the commandment is the word;" but we could hardly say the word is the commandment. The commandment is included in the word, but the word is more than the commandment. The word is the expression of the will of God, either given in direct commandment or otherwise, and we who are saved delight to keep His word. This is the approbation that the Lord puts upon Philadelphia, "Thou hast kept My word, and hast not denied My name" (Rev. 3: 8). Our Lord Himself makes this distinction between keeping His commandment and keeping His word. In the Gospel of John in one instance He says, "If ye love Me, keep my commandments" (John 14: 15), but farther on He adds, "If a man love Me, he will keep My words" (John 14: 23).

I have sometimes tried to illustrate it like this. Here is a child, a little girl in the home. She is attending school, and after school she delights to play with her young companions. One day her mother says, "My dear, when you come home from school today, there are some chores I want you to do. Dust the living-room, prepare a few things for supper. I will have to be out for a time, but when you have done these things you can go out and play." Because she is an obedient child, when she returns from school she does the things her mother has commanded her to do; she shows she loves her in this way. On another occasion she is under no such command, but coming home hears her mother speaking to the neighbor next door, and she is saying, "You know, I really do not know how I am going to get through this afternoon. I have invited company for dinner, and I am feeling so miserable and wretched that I haven't my dinner ready. There are the potatoes to peel, the vegetables to prepare, and I do not know how I can get through." In the morning she had said to the little daughter, "When you come home from school today you may have the time for play until I call you for dinner." But the dutiful child hearing this conversation between the mother and her neighbor says, "Mother dear, you go and lie down for an hour; I will peel those potatoes, I will prepare those vegetables, I will set the table and help you get the dinner." "But, my child, I told you you could play today," the mother might answer. "Oh, but I wouldn't be happy out playing knowing you were here at home feeling so badly," the child would reply. Yesterday Mary kept her mother's commands; today she is keeping her word. How it would gladden the mother's heart to have her doing these things while under no command! The renewed soul pondering over the Word of God again and again finds direct commands, certain things concerning which the Lord has spoken in a definite way, and because he loves Him it is his delight to keep those commandments. But as he continues to read, he comes across one passage after another containing no command whatever, but expressing His desires, the longings of His heart for His own people, and the loving one says, "Because Thou hast won my heart, blessed Saviour, I keep Thy words." "Whoso keepeth His word, in him verily is the love of God perfected: hereby know we that we are in Him." The word is the manifestation of what He is and of His dwelling in the believer. Thus the keeping of His word is the manifestation of the life of Christ in the one whom He has redeemed.

So the apostle adds, "He that saith he abideth in Him ought himself also so to walk, even as He walked." I cannot be all that He was; that is impossible, for He was the Holy One of God, and I in myself, although regenerated, am still a poor, failing, sinful man; but I am called upon to walk as He walked, for Christ has left us an example that we should follow His steps, and I am to glorify Him by my pilgrim behavior as I pass through this scene.

"Brethren, I write no new commandment unto you, but an old commandment which ye had from the beginning. The old commandment is the word which ye have heard from the beginning." On a previous occasion we examined that expression, "From the beginning," and we saw that it differs from the first words in the book of Genesis, "In the beginning God created the heaven and the earth" (Gen. 1: 1). That is the beginning of creation. And now this expression, "That which was from the beginning," is carrying us back to the first manifestation of God in Christ and to the ministry of our blessed Lord when He was here on earth; and so when John says, "I write no new commandment unto you, but an old commandment which ye had from the beginning," he means this: I am not telling you something strange and something new when I talk to you in this way, but I am referring you back to the Word spoken by the blessed Lord when He was here on earth in the beginning of the Christian dispensation.

False teachers had come in who were foisting new things upon the people of God, and the apostle says that the test is this: Were these things taught from the beginning?—because as we have already seen, in Christianity, "What is new is not true, and what is true is not new." We are not discovering Christianity. Christianity was a revelation committed to men by the Holy Spirit in the very beginning of the dispensation, and so John says, "I write no new commandment unto you, but an old commandment which ye had from the beginning. The old commandment is the word which ye have heard from the beginning." That is, go back to the records of our blessed Lord's life, see what He Himself has taught, and walk in obedience to His Word, for "the old commandment is the word which ye have heard from the beginning." It is not merely the summing up of the commandments when he says, "A new commandment I give unto you, that ye love one another," but it is his instruction concerning obedience to the will of God.

But now this takes on a new character. Since

Christ has died and risen from the dead, ascended to heaven, and has sent the Spirit of God to dwell in the hearts of believers, there are millions of regenerated men and women; and so to them the apostle declares, "Again, a new commandment I write unto you, which thing is true in Him and in you: because the darkness is past, and the true light now shineth." That is, the commandment is the Word of the Lord Jesus Christ. The Word was expressed in the life of Christ, but now if we are born again, the life of Christ has been communicated to us, so this thing *is true in Him and in us.* The only thing that Jesus could do when He was here on earth was the will of God. He had no other thought or desire. Well, now He dwells in us, and if we are Christians, we have His life communicated to us. So then when John speaks of His commandment, he says that it is new in this sense, because divine life is ours, and so it is true both in Him and in us. In other words, our blessed Lord in calling upon the regenerated soul to do the will of God is asking him to do the very thing that he longs to do. A mother calls in the physician to see her darling child. The little one seems to be very ill, and the doctor makes a careful examination, and says, "My dear mother, this little baby is very sick. I am going to leave you certain remedies. Do not neglect this child, do not be indifferent to its needs, watch over it very carefully, see that it

gets its medicine regularly, that it is protected
from anything that might make it worse instead
of better. Mother, do take good care of this
child!" Is he telling the mother something very
hard for her to do? "Well, Doctor," she would
say, "that is the very thing I want to do. That
is the very thing I intend to do. I love that
darling little child and nothing would induce me
to be careless in connection with it now. I long
to do the very best that I can for it." "Which
thing is true in you." The mother is told to do
the very thing her heart yearns to do. And so
the marvelous thing with us is that, "You, that
were sometime alienated, and enemies in your
mind by wicked works," now love to do the things
He asks us to do. We delight in the will of God.

"A new commandment I write unto you, which
thing is true in Him and in you: because the darkness is past, and the true light now shineth." The
word *past* does not exactly suggest the tense of
the original; what he is really saying is, "The
darkness is *passing*, and the true light is now
shining," for we see as we look out upon the
world around us or into the world within us that
it is not exactly true that the darkness is *past*.
Though the gospel of the grace of God has been
preached for 1,900 years, the darkness is not yet
fully past; there are still myriads sitting in darkness and in the shadow of death. No matter how
well I know my Lord, no matter how well I know

His Word, still it cannot be said in the fullest sense that the darkness is now past even in me, but the darkness *is passing,* and the true light is shining. Day by day I am getting to know my Lord better; day by day I am understanding His will more perfectly; but until the time comes that I leave this scene and see my blessed Saviour face to face, in me there will still be a measure of darkness, though all is light in Him.

Schiller, the German poet, said as he was dying, "I see everything clearer and clearer." And, oh, it won't be long until all the darkness will be gone, and we shall see everything in all its clearness in His own blessed presence.

In verses nine and ten the apostle speaks very seriously and very solemnly concerning something that may well exercise some of us. "He that saith he is in the light, and hateth his brother, is in darkness even until now." If you hate your brother, no matter what your profession, you are still in darkness. Now notice he does not say you may be a real Christian who has fallen into darkness; but he says, "He that saith he is in the light, and hateth his brother, is in darkness *even until now.*" He has never been anywhere else, he has never been in the light at all. You could not have divine light, you could not have the Holy Spirit who sheds abroad the love of God in the heart of a believer dwelling in you, and hate your brother. Let us test ourselves. How often you see people professing the name of Christ and yet manifesting hatred toward others.

"He that loveth his brother abideth in the light, and there is none occasion of stumbling in him," because that is the manifestation of divine life. That life is light and love, as God is light and love; and as we walk in fellowship with Him, abiding in the light, there is no occasion of stumbling, and we are manifesting the love of Christ constantly. There is no place for hatred in the heart in which the love of God has been shed abroad by the Holy Spirit.

"He that hateth his brother is in darkness, and walketh in darkness, and knoweth not whither he goeth, because that darkness hath blinded his eyes." This is the natural darkness in which all men are born: "Having the understanding darkened, being alienated from the life of God through the ignorance that is in them, because of the blindness of their heart" (Eph. 4: 18). That is the condition of man by nature. But our condemnation is not because of what we are by nature: "This is the condemnation, that light is come into the world, and men loved darkness rather than light, because their deeds were evil" (John 3: 19). Hear me; you are not responsible because you are a sinner by nature, but you are responsible if you reject the Saviour. You are not responsible because you were born in the darkness, because your understanding is darkened, but you are responsible if you reject the light that comes to you through the Word of God; light which will chase away all the darkness if you walk in it, instead of turning from its searching rays.

But if men persist in rejecting light, there may come a day when God will withdraw the light. In Jer. 13: 16 we read, "Give glory to the Lord your God, before He cause darkness, and before your feet stumble upon the dark mountains, and, while ye look for light, He turn it into the shadow of death, and make it gross darkness." That is the "strong delusion" of which we read in Thessalonians. Then there is only one step more—eternal darkness—"Wandering stars, to whom is reserved the blackness of darkness for ever" (Jude 13). "He that hateth his brother is in darkness, and walketh in darkness, and knoweth not whither he goeth, because that darkness hath blinded his eyes." But Jesus says, "I am the Light of the World: he that followeth Me shall not walk in darkness, but shall have the light of life" (John 8 :12). Have you truly trusted Him? Is He your light? Is He your life today?

> "I heard the voice of Jesus say,
>   'I am this dark world's light.
> Look unto Me, thy morn shall rise,
>   And all thy days be bright.'
> I looked to Jesus, and I found
>   In Him my star, my sun,
> And in that light of life I'll walk,
>   Till traveling days are done."

The Children of God

"I write unto you, dear children, because your sins are forgiven you for His name's sake. I write unto you, fathers, because ye have known Him that is from the beginning. I write unto you, young men, because ye have overcome the wicked one. I write unto you, little children, because ye have known the Father" (1 John 2:12, 13).

These verses introduce a distinct section of John's epistle in which he has a word of exhortation for all classes of God's children. Whatever their years of Christian life or their experience, all are addressed in verse 12 when he says, "I write unto you, dear children, because your sins are forgiven you for His name's sake." I omit purposely the word *"little,"* which you will find in our ordinary English translation and substitute the word "dear," for this reason;—the word translated *little children* in verse 12 is a very different Greek word from that translated *little children* in verse 13. The one word takes in all those who are born into the family of God and is a term of endearment, whereas the other word refers solely to those who are young. In the first instance, John is addressing all who have been redeemed to God by the precious blood of the Lord Jesus Christ, those who have been born into the great family of God by the washing of regeneration and the renewing of the Holy Spirit. They are all God's beloved children. If you have come to the place where you have given up all other ground of confidence, and are now able to say,

> "On Christ the solid rock I stand,
> All other ground is sinking sand,"

then you are numbered among the children whom John here addresses. He says, "I write unto you, children, because your sins are forgiven you for His name's sake." He has given us in an earlier verse in this epistle the basis of that forgiveness: "The blood of Jesus Christ His Son cleanseth us from all sin." There was no other way that sin could be blotted out, no other way that guilty men could be given a standing in the presence of a holy God; and no other way is needed, for yonder on Calvary's tree our blessed Lord poured forth that precious atoning blood, and, thank God,

> "Sinners plunged beneath that flood,
> Lose all their guilty stains."

These, then, are the children of God.

Men by nature are all the children of Adam, they are "alienated from the life of God through the ignorance that is in them" (Eph. 4:18), and, "Except a man be born again, he cannot see the kingdom of God" (John 3:3). Those who have trusted the Lord Jesus, those who have believed

the gospel, are already born into His family. Peter
says, "Being born again, not of corruptible seed,
but of incorruptible, by the Word of God, which
liveth and abideth forever...And this is the Word
which by the gospel is preached unto you" (1 Pet.
1 : 23-25). But now although all believers stand
on one level as the redeemed of the Lord, although
all who have trusted Christ are in one family as
the children of God, yet there are necessarily degrees of spirituality, degrees of progress in the
Christian life, and so in verse 13, the apostle divides the children of God into three classes according to the measure of their growth in grace and
in the knowledge of the Lord Jesus.

The apostle says, "I write unto you, fathers, because ye have known Him that is from the beginning. I write unto you, young men, because
ye have overcome the wicked one. I write unto
you, little children, because ye have known the
Father." It is not a question here of our actual
age and, of course, there is no question of the
sexes involved. It is not a question merely of
being a *man* in Christ as though he is not referring to our sisters at all; but these three terms,
fathers, young men, children, are used to distinguish believers according to the measure of their
growth in grace. Who are fathers? They are
those who for years have known the Lord and
walked with God, those who have grown old in
the things of Christ. Unto them John says, "I

write unto you, fathers, because ye have known Him that is from the beginning." It is quite possible to have been a Christian many years, and yet not to be in this sense a *father*. There are many who have been saved a great many years but are spiritually dwarfed because they give so little attention to spiritual things, because they give so little time to the Word of God; they are so little exercised in holy things, and know so little of the blessedness of prayer and communion with the Lord, and therefore they do not grow. But when the apostle speaks to the fathers, he is speaking to those who through long years have availed themselves of their Christian privileges, they have learned to love the Word of God, they have sought to walk with Christ, they have labored for the blessing of others, and have learned experimentally to know the blessed Lord in all His fulness, for when John says,"Ye have known Him [that is] from the beginning," it is not as though he said, "Ye have known concerning Him," or "known about Him," but "ye have known *Him*." They have lived in fellowship with Him, they have walked with Him and talked with Him, and He has become dearer and nearer and more real to them than any earthly friend. He draws very near to His own, and, if I may coin an expression, He *presences* Himself with them, and shows His hands and feet, and says, "It is I; handle Me, and see." And He bids us remember that it was for us He bore the wounds and endured the agony of the cross, in order that we might become His own. So, then, the fathers are those who have learned to know Him throughout the years; they have learned to appreciate His love, and the world has lost its power over their souls because Christ has filled the vision of the eyes of their hearts.

The next class he addresses as follows: "I write unto you, young men, because ye have overcome the wicked one." The young men are the fine stalwart Christians who, although they may not have walked with God through all the years that the fathers have, yet, having accepted Christ, have gone on with Him into spiritual maturity and have learned the secret of overcoming. In the book of Revelation we read, "They overcame by the blood of the Lamb, and by the word of their testimony" (Rev. 12:11). And so here when he says, "I write unto you, young men, because ye have overcome the wicked one," we may know that it is through their faith in that atoning blood that they have been able to turn away from the world that crucified Him, they have bade farewell to that scene that had no place for Him. Do you remember an experience like that?—a time in your life when you said,

> "My old companions, fare you well,
> I cannot go with you to hell;
> I mean with Jesus Christ to dwell,
> 　　I will go."

And you turned from the world that had rejected your Saviour, and clinging to Him you have taken His place of rejection, and though Satan has sought to terrify you by bringing before you the remembrance of past sins, you are able to plead the infinite value of His atoning blood. That is the way to overcome.

There is a third class into which he divides the family of God. These are the little ones, the babes, and to them he says, "I write unto you, little children, because you have known the Father." These are those who have not been long saved. A little while ago they were walking with the world in worldly ways and going on to the world's judgment, but they heard the gracious invitation of the loving Saviour, "Come unto Me, all ye that labor and are heavy laden, and I will give you rest" (Matt. 11: 28), and responding to His invitation, they came to Him, came with all their sins and their grief, and found how true a friend Jesus is to those who trust Him, and now though they do not know much else, they know the Father. It is to the little babes in Christ that the Holy Spirit is given.

God does not wait until we become mature Christians before the Holy Spirit is given to us. "Having begun in the Spirit, are ye now made perfect by the flesh?" (Gal. 3: 3). We *began* in the Spirit; we received the Spirit of God as soon as we believed in Jesus, and He teaches us to cry, "Abba

Father." And whereas a while ago these babes in Christ belonged to the world and were led by the god of this world, now they have been weaned away from it all to God Himself, and they look up into His blessed face and are able to say, "My Father." There is a great deal for the babes to learn. Many varied experiences are still ahead of them, there are wonderful truths yet to be opened up, but they are as truly accepted in the Beloved as the fathers are, they are as truly cleansed from every sin as the young men who "have overcome the wicked one," and all these three classes are included in the one term, *children*—"I write unto you, children, because your sins are forgiven you for His name's sake."

How to Overcome

"I have written unto you, fathers, because ye have known Him that is from the beginning. I have written unto you, young men, because ye are strong and the word of God abideth in you, and ye have overcome the wicked one. Love not the world, neither the things that are in the world. If any man love the world, the love of the Father is not in him. For all that is in the world, the lust of the flesh, and the lust of the eyes, and the pride of life, is not of the Father, but is of the world. And the world passeth away, and the lust thereof: but he that doeth the will of God abideth for ever" (1 John 2:14-17).

Beginning with verse 14 John goes on to give a word of encouragement, a word of warning, a word of exhortation, to each of these classes, so he mentions them all again in order. To the fathers he says, "I have written unto you, fathers, because ye have known Him that is from the beginning." He does not add anything to that; it is exactly what he said before. Why does he not add anything? Because you cannot add anything to that. That is the climax of Christian experience—"Ye have known Him that is from the beginning."

There are not many fathers. People may be very old in Christ and yet not be properly designated *fathers* in this sense, for many very old in

years are still very carnal in their experience
and know very little of true fellowship with Him.
Paul earnestly prayed, "That I may know Him,
and the power of His resurrection, and the fellowship of His sufferings, being made conforma-
able unto His death" (Phil. 3:10). It is this that
constitutes one a father in Christ. This is the
fullest Christian maturity, and this comes through
a life of fellowship with Him who "is from the
beginning."

We have noticed that this expression, "From
the beginning," is not the same as, "In the beginning." You and I could not know Him in the
beginning; God the Father alone knew Him in the
past eternity. "In the beginning was the Word,
and the Word was with God, and the Word was
God" (John 1:1). But when we say, "From the
beginning," that means from the time He became
incarnate here on earth. Now John says, "Ye
have known Him that is from the beginning."
Sweet to trace His toiling footsteps as He walks
the sands of earth, to see Him in His wonderful
perfection down here, God manifest in the flesh,
and to know Him now as the One who passed
through death, who was raised by the glory of the
Father, and has ascended to heaven, and sits exalted at God's right hand, our great High Priest,
our Advocate. Does your soul long to know Him,
do you seek to get better acquainted with Him
through the years? There is only one way that

you will ever become a father in Christ. There are a great many people quite clear as to certain great doctrines, very pronounced as to where they stand on the fundamental and modernistic controversy, they have very rigid ideas as to how the people of God should meet together; and yet there is one thing very evident, they do not know Christ in this intimate relationship that is indicated here.

How do you get to know a person? By living with him day by day. How do you get to know Christ? By living in intimate fellowship with Him throughout the days and years. You know Him as you look up to Him through the clouds of sorrow and He ministers so graciously to the heart. You know Him when in the midst of the joys of life; you put Christ first and find your chief joy and gladness in Him. To know Him! This is to be a father in Christ. He does not add a thing to that, not a word of exhortation. Why? Because what could be added? Think of going to one to whom Christ is everything, and saying, "My brother, let me give you a kindly word of warning, a word of admonition: try to be very careful that you do not drift off into the ways of the world." "Oh," he would say, "the world has lost its charm for me since Christ has filled the vision of my soul." When Christ becomes the one Object of the heart, nothing more can be added to that. That is what delivers from the power of the world, that is what saves from carnality, that is what keeps from jealousy and envy and everything else of the flesh. When Christ is all in all these things will not be.

But now the apostle turns in the second place to another class who have not gone on into the depths of experience that the fathers have, and yet are strong vigorous Christians. He says, "I have written unto you, young men, because ye are strong, and the Word of God abideth in you, and ye have overcome the wicked one." When he spoke to them previously, he simply said, "I write unto you, young men, because ye have overcome the wicked one." But now he gives us the secret of that overcoming : Not strong in their own power but in the Lord and in the power of His might, and because "the Word of God abideth in you." There are people who spend the greater part of the week occupied solely with the things of earth, things that in themselves are very right and legitimate. Once a week they come together for Bible study or worship, and say, "How refreshing and helpful !" It is like folk coming for one good meal a week. That is not the way to be strong. "I write unto you, young men, because ye are strong, and the Word of God abideth in you, and ye have overcome the wicked one." It is the Word of God first thing in the morning, the Word of God all day long, and the Word of God the last thing at night. You go to bed with the Word of God in your mind and you will wake up with the Word of God in your mind. It is the Word of God that keeps from the power of the enemy all the hours of the day. Some say, "I do not think this is possible." But it is possible, and many have proven it. Somebody said to me once concerning a fellow-laborer, "I like your friend; he seems to be just a walking Bible." That was because that man was constantly feeding on it.

I knew a blacksmith who was so eager to become a man of God that he used to cut his Bible into sections, and tie one up with a piece of string right by the side of his forge, and then he would pull a page of it off and tack it up before him, and as he worked away at the blacksmith shop, he would be reading the Word. Was it any wonder that three years later God called that man away from the blacksmith shop into active Christian service? For forty years he has been an evangelist, leading many to the Lord Jesus Christ. Another man whom I knew was a printer, and he had his Bible on a little stand before him, and as he worked away on one of those great circular presses, he had his heart set on the things of God. He would get a verse and meditate on it as he worked, and then get another, and another. It was not long until God took that man away from the printing-press and sent him out preaching. He always said he got his theological seminary training standing at his printing-press.

"Because the Word of God abideth in you." You know there are many Christians who think of the Word of God as something to take up an extra hour or so when they have nothing else to do; but one will never grow that way. What little strength you get from that hour is all used up when you are occupied with other things. You do not get anywhere that way. But when the Word of God is the supreme thing in your life, and everything else is made to fit into that, you will grow, and become a strong Christian.

The world is bidding for these fine young Christians. The world and its allurements are all about them, and the devil would do a great deal to trip up earnest Christians like these. There are some Christians the devil scarcely bothers about, but there are others out and out for God, and Satan is near with his snares and allurements, tripping them on this hand and that, and if they flee from one thing he has another temptation for them; and so the exhortation comes, "Love not the world, neither the things of the world. If any man love the world, the love of the Father is not in him. For all that is in the world, the lust of the flesh, and the lust of the eyes, and the pride of life, is not of the Father, but is of the world. And the world passeth away, and the lust thereof: but he that doeth the will of God abideth for ever."

What is this world that we are not to love? It is not the globe as such. The globe itself has nothing in it that can hurt our souls. We can love nature; we do not need to be afraid of a beautiful view or a lovely flower. I have seen some Christians who had an idea that John meant we were not to enjoy the world of nature. I said to one, "Isn't that a beautiful rose bush?" and he replied, "I am not interested in roses; I am not of this world." That is not the world that is spoken of. This universe is but the expression of the Father's wisdom and goodness.

> "Heaven above is softer blue,
>   Earth beneath is sweeter green!
> Something lives in ev'ry hue
>   Christless eyes have never seen:
> Birds with gladder songs o'erflow,
>   Flow'rs with deeper beauties shine,
> Since I know, as now I know,
>   I am His, and He is mine!"

My Lord loved the lilies of the field. He drew attention to the beauties of nature, they stirred His own soul, and He would have His people see in them the evidences of the wisdom and goodness of the Father. But what, then, is the world? It is that system that man has built up in this scene, in which he is trying to make himself happy without God. You get it away back in Genesis, where Cain went out from the presence of the Lord and builded a city, and there what we call the world really began. It was a wonderful world; they were exercised in all kinds of arts, sciences, business, and pleasure, anything and everything to make them happy without God; but it ended in corruption and violence, and God had to sweep the whole thing away with a flood. The principles of the world that caused the corruption and violence before the flood were carried into the ark in the hearts of some of Noah's children. They brought the world into the ark, and when the new world was started after the judgment of the flood, they brought the world out of the ark with them, and again set it up.

When some think of the world, they think of things that are abominable and vile and corrupt, the old-fashioned saloon and gambling-place, and all kinds of violence. Things like that hold little to attract the Christian heart, but the world they need to beware of is the world of culture, the world that appeals to their esthetic nature. That world has no more place for the Christian than the corrupt, abominable world in the slums of our great cities. Do not imagine that if your world is a cultured world consisting of devotees of the arts and sciences, that you are safe and free from worldliness. Even the business world may become just as great a snare as any other. But you ask, "Do not we have to go into business?" Yes, Jesus says, "I pray not that Thou shouldest take them out of the world, but that Thou shouldest keep them from the evil" (John 17: 15). In all these things we have to watch against the evils of the world.

What is then the lust of the flesh (the gratification of the flesh), the lust of the eye (the desires of the unregenerate soul), the pride of life? I remember when I was a young Christian, my world against which I had to guard most was the world of polite literature. I used to love it, its poetry, its essays, its wonderful books, and I appreciate them yet in a certain sense, but I had to remember this, that if ever these things came in between my soul and my love for this blessed Book, I had to turn away from them and give my time and attention to this Book, and so it is with many things. There was a young lady with great musical ability preparing to go on the concert stage when the Lord saved her. She said one day, "You know I have made a wonderful discovery; my very love for music is coming in between my soul and Christ," and that young woman for eight years would not touch a musical instrument, for she was afraid she would become so absorbed that she would not enjoy the things of God. The time came when she said, "I cannot enjoy music for its own sake, but I can use it as a vehicle to bless the souls of men," and she gave her talent to Christ, and He used it in attracting people to hear the gospel. No matter what it is, if you lay it down at Jesus' feet and use it for Him, you do not need to be afraid of it. But do not put your work before Jesus Christ. Sometimes a fine house is "the world." Here is a Christian, and while he is little in his own eyes and has not much means, he lives in a quiet little home, but the Lord trusts him with a good deal of money, and he immediately says, "I must have a better house now; I must have some style about me; I must have magnificent furniture and draperies." What for? Is he any more comfortable? He can eat just three meals a day, he can sleep in just one bed at a time, and sit in just one chair at a time, but he feels he must impress people.

Beauty, too, can get in between you and Christ, and it will prove to be "the world" if one is not careful. "For all that is in the world, the lust of the flesh, and the lust of the eyes, and the pride of life, is not of the Father, but is of the world."

What is "the pride of life?" The ostentation of living, trying to make an appearance before others, the vain-glory of the world. I think sometimes if some Christians took two-thirds of the money that they put into a mansion down here, and invested it in sending the gospel to a lost world, they would have a much finer mansion up there. "Love not the world, neither the things that are in the world . . . The world passeth away, and the lust thereof." I was passing along the street the other day with a friend, and he said, as he pointed out one house after another, "There is an awful lot of tragedy connected with that house. A man built this great home for his beautiful wife, and suddenly she died. Here is a house

that had much money put into it, but there was
a suicide in the family, and now no one cares to
live in it." There is no real joy in these things.
As Christians, ours are the only joys that last
forever; ours are the things that will never pass
away, and yet to think that we can be so foolish
and invest so much in that which is simply fleet-
ing and will leave us dissatisfied and unhappy at
last.

"But he that doeth the will of God abideth for
ever." In obedience to His will there is lasting
joy, there is endless gladness. In the light of
that, who would not say,

> "Take the world, but give me Jesus,
>   All earth's joys are but in name,
> But His love abideth ever,
>   Through eternal years the same."

Have you made your choice, Christian? You
made your choice once when you turned from sin
to Christ. Have you made the other choice? Have
you turned from the world to Christ? There is
many a one who has trusted Jesus as his Saviour
from judgment, who has never learned to know
Him as the rejected One with whom he is called
to walk in hallowed fellowship.

No one can ever put this world beneath his feet
until he has found a better world above. When
your heart is taken up with that world, it is an
easy thing to heed the exhortation, "Love not the
world, neither the things that are in the world."

God's Little Children—Their Privileges and Dangers

"Little children, it is the last time: and as ye have heard that antichrist shall come, even now are there many antichrists; whereby we know that it is the last time. They went out from us, but they were not of us; for if they had been of us, they would no doubt have continued with us: but they went out, that they might be made manifest that they were not all of us. But ye have an unction from the Holy One, and ye know all things. I have not written unto you because ye know not the truth, but because ye know it, and that no lie is of the truth. Who is a liar but he that denieth that Jesus is the Christ? He is antichrist, that denieth the Father and the Son. Whosoever denieth the Son, the same hath not the Father: [but] he that acknowledgeth the Son hath the Father also. Let that therefore abide in you, which ye have heard from the beginning. If that which ye have heard from the beginning shall remain in you, ye also shall continue in the Son, and in the Father. And this is the promise that He hath promised us, even eternal life. These things have I written unto you concerning them that seduce you. But the anointing which ye have received of Him abideth in you, and ye need not that any man teach you: but as the same anointing teacheth you of all things, and is truth, and is no lie, and even as it hath taught you, ye shall abide in Him" (1 John 2: 18-27).

We have been noticing that the Holy Spirit in addressing the family of God has divided it into three classes, according to the measure of their growth in grace. We have already considered what the Lord has to say to the fathers in Christ and to the young men, the stalwart, mature Christians. Now we come to consider His message to God's little children.

"Little children, it is the last time: and as ye have heard that antichrist shall come, even now are there many antichrists; whereby we know that it is the last time." The word translated *little children* here, as I pointed out on a previous occasion, is very different from the word translated *little children* in the first part of verse 12. There it is a term of affection, and implies all who are born into God's family, God's bairns, to use a well-known Scotch term, all His dear children. But these dear children, as we have seen, are of different degrees of spiritual experience, and they are divided into the three classes given in verse 13, the fathers who have known the Lord for many years and have walked with Him and talked with Him and drunk deep of His love, the young men in whom the Word of God abides and who have overcome the wicked one, and now the little children, the babes in Christ, those who have not been long saved, or, though some of them may have been saved for years, have not been well nourished, have not been builded up in Christ, and though perhaps they ought to be in one of the other classes are still God's little children, still babes. They are passing through the world in which there are a great many adverse influences seeking to turn them away from the simplicity that is in Christ, and so the apostle immediately warns them, and singularly enough, he warns them against the spirit of antichrist. "Ye have heard that antichrist shall come, even now are there many antichrists; whereby we know that it is the last time." John is the only writer who uses that particular term; other terms are used in other parts of Scripture;—the Idol Shepherd, the Lawless One, the Wilful King, the Son of Perdition, the Man of Sin, the False Prophet, and the one who shall come in his own name. These different terms describe the same person, the one who shall arise in the days of the great tribulation and lead guilty apostate Christendom and Judaism farther away from God than they are at the present time.

The antichrist has not yet appeared, but the spirit of antichrist is in the world, and "even now are there many antichrists." The spirit of antichrist is the putting of man in the place of God and His Christ—self-worship, humanism—and the babes need to be warned against this. The worst of it is that many of the advocates of these unholy systems were once numbered among the Christian company. They took their places at the communion-table, had fellowship outwardly with the people of God, went through Christian baptism, but now have turned away from the Christianity of this blessed Book, from the simplicity that is in Christ, and deny the precious blood that once they confessed. In the light of Scripture testimony which says, "My sheep hear My voice, and I know them, and they follow Me: and I give unto them eternal life; and they shall never perish, neither shall any man pluck them out of My hand" (John 10: 27, 28), how are we to account for people who have for years walked in the Christian company and seemed to be just as real as any other professed believers, but now count "the blood of the covenant, wherewith they were sanctified, an unholy thing, and have done despite unto the Spirit of grace" (Heb. 10: 29), and spurned the love of our Lord Jesus Christ? The answer is, "They were not altogether of us, or they would have continued with us."

I remember how my heart was stirred after the war as I read of one of our great American preachers, great from the standpoint of ability, culture, and rhetoric, but who knew nothing of the saving grace of God. He said that after he had been to Europe and after his experience in the trenches, he threw overboard the doctrine of blood-atonement through the precious sacrifice of our Lord Jesus Christ, gave up the doctrine of the deity of Christ, and scoffed at His virgin birth and His resurrection. How could so great a preacher repudiate these things? We are not left to speculate about this, for the explanation is given by the Holy Spirit Himself in verse 19,

"They went out from us, but they were not of us; for if they had been of us, they would no doubt have continued with us; but they went out, that they might be made manifest that they were not all of us." Their going out made it manifest that they were not genuinely of the believers. They bore the Christian name, they joined some Christian church, the name of the Father and of the Son and of the Holy Spirit was called over them in holy baptism, they took the bread and the wine at the table of the Lord, but He who seeth not as man seeth said, "The hand of him that betrayeth Me is with Me on the table" (Luke 22: 21). He knew what Judas really was, and so said, "Have not I chosen you twelve, and one of you *is* a devil?" (John 6: 70). He was never anything else.

God knows who are the unreal among His people today. He knows all who mingle with the people of God, who profess the name of Christ, but have never known the blessing of regenerating grace, never bowed in repentance at the cross of Christ, who have never been washed from their sins in the Saviour's precious blood. The hardest thing in the world to do is to attempt to live a Christian life and meet the obligations of a Christian, when you have no Christian life to live. As well might one of the beasts of the field set himself up in a mansion and try to live the life of a millionaire human being, as for an unregenerated sinner to try to live the life of a Christian. "Ye must be born again." "Except a man be born again, he cannot see the kingdom of God" (John 3: 3). And so here were these men mingling with Christians and outwardly looking like them, but John says, "They were not of us;" they were not genuine. Oh, may each one of us search our hearts in the presence of God and ask the questions, "Have I really faced my sins in the light of the cross of Christ; have I truly turned to God in repentance, owning my guilt, acknowledging my iniquity, and fled for refuge to the hope set before me in the gospel? Have I the evidence of a regenerate soul—do I love the brethren, do I love the commandments of God, is the Word sweet to me, do I delight to feed upon it, is it my joy to serve Him, or, after all, are these things to me but a weariness of the flesh?" I am persuaded, and I say it in all charity, that there are tens of thousands of people today whose names are on the church-rolls of this and other lands who have never had their names enrolled in the Lamb's Book of Life—tens of thousands of people struggling to live a Christian life, and making a complete failure of it because they have never yet been born again.

When that great revival comes for which many have been praying for so long, if it pleases God to send it ere the return of His blessed Son, one of the first evidences of it will be that people who

have used the Christian name and passed for
Christian workers will begin to find out that they
themselves have never been converted, and there
will be a breaking down before God, a confessing
of their sins and judging of their iniquities and
selfishness. What a fearful thing never to find
out the truth until in the day of doom it is too late
to rectify the error!

Here were these people going on with the
Christian company, "But," says the Spirit of God,
"they were not of us," and so by and by they went
out, and when outside they became the worst opponents of those who stood for the truth of God.
There is no one who hates the gospel like the
man who at one time professed to be saved but
afterward turned to a life of sin because there
was no reality there. These were the antichrists
against whom John warned the little children in
his day.

But now what is their resource under such circumstances? Look at verses 20 and 21. "But ye
have an anointing from the Holy One, and ye
know all things. I have not written unto you because ye know not the truth, but because ye know
it, and that no lie is of the truth." He says, "Ye
know all things"—not actually every detail, but
potentially. You have dwelling in you the One
who does know, and therefore you need not be
carried away by any form of error. What is it
then that these little babes have as their resource?

The Spirit of God and the Word of God. They have the Spirit of God dwelling in them as the anointing, the Word of God in their hearts to open the truth to them. When people come with their false teachings that deny the atoning blood, that set to one side the blessed Christ of God and make a great deal of human attainment, the little babes in Christ turn back to the Word of God, and the Spirit of God dwelling in them opens the Word to them and thus preserves them from error.

The story is told by a well-known English minister, now with his Lord, how, years ago, one night when he was just ready to retire there came a knock at his door, and when he went downstairs, he found at the door a poor, wretched little girl, dripping wet. She had come through the storm, and she said, "Are you the minister?" "Yes," he said, "I am." He was at that time one who had turned away from the simplicity of the gospel. "Well, won't you come and get my mother in?" she asked. The minister said, "Why, I was just about to retire, and besides it is hardly seemly for me to go out and get your mother in. If she is drunk, you can get a policeman to get her in. He has his oilskins on and is prepared for the storm." "Oh," she said, "you don't understand! My mother is not out in the storm, she is not drunk, she is at home and is dying, and she is afraid to die: she is afraid she is going to be lost

forever, and she wants to go to heaven and
doesn't know how, and I told her I would get a
minister to get her in." He asked where she
lived, and she told him of a district so vile that
even in the daytime respectable people did not go
there without a policeman accompanying them.
"Why," he said, "I cannot go down there tonight,"
and subconsciously he said, "It would be all my
reputation is worth to be seen with a girl like
this in that district in the middle of the night;
no, I cannot go. As the preacher of this great
and important church, what would my people
think if it should get into the papers?" To the
girl he said, "I will tell you what to do. You go
down and get the man who is running the Rescue
Mission; he will be glad to help you." He said he
felt ashamed as he said it, but thought his reputation had to be maintained. "He may be a good
man," she said, "but I don't know him. I told my
mother I would get a real minister, and I want
you to come and get her in. Come quickly; she's
dying." "I couldn't stand the challenge in those
eyes," the preacher said, "I felt so ashamed, and
so said to her, 'Very well, I will come.'" He
went upstairs and dressed and put on his great-
coat, and then the girl led him down through the
city and into the slum district, into an old house,
up a rickety stairway and along a long dark hall
into a little room, and there lay the poor woman.
"I have gotten the preacher of the biggest church

in the city," said the girl; "he will get you in; he
didn't want to come, but he's come. You tell him
what you want, and do just what he tells you to
do." The woman looked up and said, "Oh, sir,
can you do anything for a poor sinner? All my
life I have been a wicked woman, and I am going
to hell, but I don't want to go there; I want to be
saved, I want to go to heaven. Tell me what I
can do." The doctor said, relating the incident in
a large meeting, "I stood there looking down at
that poor anxious face, and thought, Whatever
will I tell her? I had been preaching in my own
church on salvation by character, by ethical culture, by reformation, and I thought, I can't tell
her about salvation by character, for she hasn't
any; I can't tell her about salvation by ethical culture, for there's no time for culture, and besides
she most likely wouldn't know what I meant; I
can't tell her about salvation by reformation, for
she has gone too far to reform. Then it came to
me, Why not tell her what your mother used to
tell you? She's dying, and it can't hurt her, even
though it does her no good. And so I said, 'My
poor woman, God is very gracious, and the Bible
says, 'God so loved the world, that He gave His
only begotten Son, that whosoever believeth in
Him should not perish, but have everlasting life'
(John 3: 16). She said, 'Does it say that in the
Bible? My! This ought to help get me in. But,
sir, my sins! What about my sins?' It was amaz-

ing the way the verses came to me, verses I had
learned years ago and never used, and I said, 'The
blood of Jesus Christ His Son cleanseth us from
all sin' (1 John 1: 7). 'All sin?' she said: 'Does
it really say that the blood will cleanse me from
all sin? That ought to get me in.' 'This is a faithful saying and worthy of all acceptation, that
Christ Jesus came into the world to save sinners;
of whom I am chief' (1 Tim. 1: 15). 'Well,' she
said, 'If the chief got in, I can come. Pray for
me!' I knelt down and prayed with that poor
woman and *got her in,* and while I was getting
her in, I got myself in. We two poor sinners, the
minister and the dying harlot, were saved together in that little room."

Oh, those messages that have nothing whatever
that will help a poor, guilty, hell-bound sinner,
what abominations they are in the sight of God!
But, thank God, He has given His little children
the blessed Holy Spirit to guide, to direct, to instruct, to open to them the truth, and through the
truth they are kept from the power of the evil
one.

Then we read, "Who is a liar but he that denieth that Jesus is the Christ? He is antichrist,
that denieth the Father and the Son." John
comes out with strong language. "Whosoever denieth the Son, the same hath not the Father: *but
he that acknowledgeth the Son hath the Father
also.*" The words placed in italics in our Author-

ized Version generally represent words *not* found in the Greek, but since the New Testament was translated in 1611 many other manuscripts have been discovered, and they all contain these words.

"Let that therefore abide in you which ye have heard from the beginning. If that which ye have heard from the beginning shall remain in you, ye also shall continue in the Son, and in the Father." If that gospel has not gripped your heart, you will some day drift away as others have drifted away. "These things have I written unto you concerning them that seduce you. But the anointing which ye have received of Him abideth in you, and ye need not that any man teach you: but as the same anointing teacheth you of all things, and is truth, and is no lie, and even as it hath taught you, ye shall abide in Him." They were not to be dependent upon any human wisdom, for they had the Word opened to them by the Holy Spirit.

This, then, is the comfort, the stay, the protection of God's little children. They may not know very much, but they know Christ, and they have the Holy Spirit dwelling in them and the Word of God to instruct them. May we all learn to value what God so graciously has committed to us.

The Father's Love and Christ's Appearing

"And now, little children, abide in Him; that, when He shall appear, we may have confidence, and not be ashamed before Him at His coming. If ye know that He is righteous, ye know that every one that doeth righteousness is born of Him. Behold, what manner of love the Father hath bestowed upon us, that we should be called the sons of God: therefore the world knoweth us not, because it knew Him not. Beloved, now are we the sons of God, and it doth not yet appear what we shall be: but we know that, when He shall appear, we shall be like Him; for we shall see Him as He is. And every man that hath this hope in Him purifieth himself, even as He is pure" (1 John 2: 28, 29—3: 1-3).

In verse 28 John comes back to the word with which he began in verse 12, and uses once more the term, *dear children,* to address all the family of God irrespective of maturity or immaturity, of youth or age, and says, "And now, dear children, abide in Him." To abide in Him is to live in fellowship with Him. It is one thing to be in Him, as having life in Him, but it is another thing to abide in Him as enjoying communion with Him. Many there are who have life in Christ, but are not happy in His presence. They permit something to come into the life that hinders fellowship.

You know how it is in a family, when the children are in harmony with the father and mother they give their parents satisfaction and there is peace and joy and fellowship, but if one of the children is out of touch with the rest and has been wilful and wayward, disobedient and ungrateful, some way or another there is a sense of a barrier between that child and the parents. Not that the parents do not love the child as much as ever, but he realizes that his own behavior has come in the way of fellowship. So it is with the children of God, and John says, "And now, dear children, abide in Him; that, when He shall appear, we may have confidence, and not be ashamed before Him at His coming."

It is at the appearing of our Lord Jesus Christ that our rewards are going to be given out. "Behold, I come quickly; and My reward is with Me, to give every man according as his work shall be" (Rev. 22: 12). In view of that, the apostle says, "Abide in Him; that, when He shall appear, we may have confidence, and not be ashamed before Him at His coming." In 2 Cor. 5: 10 we read, "We must all appear (or be manifest) before the judgment-seat of Christ)." The apostle is desirous that when the day of manifestation comes, "we may have confidence and not be ashamed before Him." Notice the pronoun. He is addressing the children, and you might expect him to say, "That, when He shall appear, *you* may have confidence, and not be ashamed before Him at His coming." You see, he is speaking as a servant of Christ, addressing those whom he has led to Christ or whom he has sought to help in the ways of God. He speaks for all Christ's servants as he addresses all God's people, and says, as it were, "We are accountable, we have a tremendous sense of responsibility in regard to you." You remember how another apostle spoke of Christ's undershepherds as those who had heavy responsibility, and says, "They watch for your souls, as they that must give account; that they may do it with joy, and not with grief: for that is unprofitable for you" (Heb. 13: 17).

"Abide in Him; that, when He shall appear, *we* may have confidence, and not be ashamed before Him at His coming." I remember some years ago trying to speak on this text in connection with another subject. I was addressing a crowded house in Detroit, and after dismissing the audience at the close of the meeting, I saw a young woman on the left side of the church push her way across to the right side, and she threw herself weeping into the arms of a beautiful Christian woman, saying, "Oh, Mrs. M——, will you forgive me? Can you forgive me?" The woman tried to quiet and soothe her, and said, "It is not I who needs to forgive you; if you have sinned, you have done so against the Lord. Go to Him." "Oh, but," the young woman said, "you led me to

Christ, and you were my Sunday School teacher, and you have tried to lead me on. I used to be so happy as a young Christian, and then I fell in love with an unconverted man, and you warned me that it was not the right thing for a Christian girl to do; you told me fully about the unequal yoke, but I said, 'I will soon bring him around so that he will become a Christian,' but it hasn't worked that way. He has taken me his way, away from the Church of God, into the world. This is the first meeting I have attended for months. I have been going with him to the theatre and to the dance and have lost out, and it never dawned on me how ashamed you would be of me at the judgment-seat of Christ. I want to be right with God." I saw that dear woman take her into a side room for a time of prayer, and when they came out their faces were shining with the light that is never seen on sea or land.

It is one thing to have come to Christ, it is another thing to behave yourself in such a way that those who led you to Christ and have watched over your soul can give account with joy in that great day. Sometimes even here on earth I have been a little ashamed, for I have gone into certain places and met some one who did not seem to have the marks of Christian devotedness, and then somebody said, "Don't you know so and so?" "I am not sure that I do," I have replied. "Well, he is one of your converts." I understand that they meant that he had professed to be converted in one of my meetings, but he had not been going on.

Nothing gives a true servant of Christ greater joy, after the conversion of sinners, than to see those he has won for the Saviour glorifying Him in their lives.

You remember when you first came to trust in Christ. What have you been doing since? What has He been getting out of your life? Have you been playing fast and loose with the world, trying to carry water on both shoulders? You cannot do this without going astray. If you have been redeemed to God by the precious blood of Christ and regenerated by the grace of His Holy Spirit, let Him have the best of your life, abide in Him, and then in that coming day when the servants of Christ come up before the judgment-seat to be rewarded according to their service, they won't be ashamed of you. Think of D. L. Moody standing before the Lord, and saying, "Lord, behold, I and the children whom Thou hast given me," and then think of some of them as they stand there saying to themselves, "Oh, I wish I had lived more in accord with what my dear father in Christ taught me."

In verse 29 John reminds us of what should characterize those that have been born of God, "If ye know that He is righteous, ye know that every one that doeth righteousness is born of Him." Do not be content to say, "I have trusted Christ and

have been made the righteousness of God in Him."
When God justifies a man by faith, He then pro-
ceeds to make that man just by the inworking of
His Holy Spirit. He does not justify people by
faith and leave them in an unjust condition, but
every one that is born of God doeth righteousness, loves righteousness, seeks to walk in righteousness. Let us test ourselves by some of these
things, and see whether or not we are professing
to be Christians when we have never known
righteousness.

To those that are saved what beautiful words
are written in the opening verses of the next
chapter. First comes the "manner of love that the
Father hath bestowed upon us, that we should be
called the sons of God: therefore the world
knoweth us not, because it knew Him not." You
see this is something different from the general
love of John 3: 16, "For God so loved the *world,*
that He gave His only begotten Son, that whosoever believeth in Him should not perish, but have
everlasting life." That is infinite love to lost men
everywhere. If you are out of Christ, be assured
of this: the love of God goes out to you and He
has commended His love toward you in that while
you were yet a sinner Christ died for you. But
you know there is something sweeter, there is
something even more precious than that, but it is
not for you until you trust in Christ, but if you
have already trusted in Him, then you can enter

into the Father's love. "Behold, what manner of love the Father hath bestowed upon us." It is the *children who are addressed,* not *sons.* It is a rather singular thing that so often in our Authorized Version, in the translation of John's writings, we have the word *sons* where it should be *children.* "That we should be called the *children* of God." And because we are the children of God "the world knoweth us not, because it knew Him not."

If you have the Revised Version you will notice that there are three words added which were found in some old manuscripts which were not known when the King James' Version was translated, "Behold, what manner of love the Father hath bestowed upon us, that we should be called children of God, *and we are.*" It is not that we hope to be, but we are. Are you clear about that? If you are, you will never sing,

> " 'Tis a point I long to know,
>   Oft it causes anxious thought,
>   Do I love my Lord or no?
>   Am I His, or am I not?"

I would not dishonor my Lord by singing words like that when I read, "Rejoice, because your names are written in heaven." I do not wonder that those words dropped out of some of the manuscripts, for they must have been too much for some of the folk copying them. Therefore, be-

cause we are, because we have been born of God,
have been regenerated, the world does not understand; it knows us not because it knew Him not.
If it did not know Him, we cannot expect it to
recognize us. Because He passed through this
scene a stranger and a pilgrim, we too go through
it as strangers and pilgrims, refusing to look at
things from the world's standpoint.

"Beloved, now are we the children of God"—
not we hope to find that we are such when we get
to heaven but—"*Now* are we the children of God."
But then we find that there is something that we
are waiting for. "It doth not yet appear what we
shall be: but we know that, when He shall appear, we shall be like Him; for we shall see Him
as He is." This is our great expectation, and
soon every believer will be fully conformed to His
blessed image. What a wonderful day that will
be! But right now God looks at His people as
they are going to be when He gets through with
them. We look at each other as we are now, and
get so discouraged with ourselves and with one
another, but God is looking at us as we shall be
when we see our blessed Lord and are changed
into His glorious image.

A story is told of an artist who had in his
mind the conception of a great picture which he
was going to paint. He stretched his vast canvas
straight across one side of his large studio, put
up the scaffolding, brought the large, thick

brushes, and prepared the paint. It looked like
a job of house painting. He painted with great
sweeps of his brush as he put in the background.
Day after day he would walk back and forth putting a daub of gray here, a daub of blue there, and
some black there, and one day he came down
from the scaffolding to look at it. He kept moving back, and back, and back. A visitor had come
in unnoticed, and as the artist moved backward
he bumped right into him. He turned around and
said, "Why, you here? I didn't know you had
come in. What do you think of that picture?
That is going to be the masterpiece of my life.
Isn't it magnificent?" The other said, "I don't
see anything there but a lot of great daubs of
paint." "Oh, I forgot," said the artist; "you can
see only what is there, while I can see the picture
as it is going to be." The blessed Lord sees us as
we are going to be when we see Him, for then
we shall be just like Him. Even now on earth,
"We all, with open face beholding as in a glass
the glory of the Lord, are changed into the same
image from glory to glory, even as by the Spirit
of the Lord" (2 Cor. 3: 18). And when we see
Him as He is, we shall become just like Him.

"And every man that hath this hope in Him
purifieth himself, even as He is pure." It is literally, "Every man that hath this hope *set on Him*"
—looking on to the coming of the Lord Jesus, the
blessed hope of His return. I do not know any

incentive to godly living like the hope of the coming again of the Lord Jesus Christ. People must be weaned away from the world by heart-occupation with the coming Saviour. You cannot be taken up with Him, the coming One, and be taken up with the world at the same time, for it is impossible not to be weaned away from the world when your heart is occupied with Him. You do not have to give up the world for Jesus' sake. The fact of the matter is that:

"The things of earth will grow strangely dim
In the light of His glory and grace."

When you are looking on to His return, you cannot enjoy the things of the world that crucified Him; and conversely, if you are a Christian and trying to enjoy the world, forgetting that you are called to be separate from the world, you cannot enjoy Christ. You cannot enjoy Christ and the world at the same time. In the fly-leaf of John Bunyan's Bible he had written,

"This Book will keep you from sin,
Or sin will keep you from this Book."

And so we may say, occupation with Christ will save you from worldliness, or worldliness will hide the glory of His wonderful face. "Every man that hath this hope in Him purifieth himself, even as He is pure."

The Two Natures

"Whosoever committeth sin transgresseth also the law: for sin is the transgression of the law. And ye know that He was manifested to take away our sins; and in Him is no sin. Whosoever abideth in Him sinneth not: whosoever sinneth hath not seen Him, neither known Him. Little children, let no man deceive you: he that doeth righteousness is righteous, even as He is righteous. He that committeth sin is of the devil; for the devil sinneth from the beginning. For this purpose the Son of God was manifested, that He might destroy the works of the devil. Whosoever is born of God doth not commit sin; for his seed remaineth in him: and he cannot sin, because he is born of God. In this the children of God are manifest, and the children of the devil: whosoever doeth not righteousness is not of God, neither he that loveth not his brother" (1 John 3: 4-10).

We have in the fourth verse what purports to be a definition of sin. Just what is sin? You remember the little lad who when his Sunday School teacher asked him this question, said, "I think it is anything you like to do." After all, that is not so far wrong, because in our natural state we are so utterly out of touch with God that we like to do those things that are contrary to His holy will. The definition here given, "Whosoever committeth sin transgresseth also the law: for sin is the transgression of the law," is not very accurate in our Version. It should read, "Whosoever committeth sin committeth lawlessness, for sin is lawlessness." In other words, sin does not consist merely in the transgression of a definitely revealed law. Our Authorized Version might seem to indicate this, but if we turn back to Romans, we find that we are distinctly told that "where no law is, there is no transgression" (Romans 4: 15), but "until the law sin was in the world."

If sin is the transgression of the law, how could sin have been in the world before the law was given? If we accept the more accurate rendering, all is clear. "Sin is lawlessness," and that is the very essence of sin. It is insubjection to God, taking my own way. That is what we all do naturally. Isaiah says, "All we like sheep have gone astray; we have turned every one to his own way; and the Lord hath laid on Him the iniquity of us all" (Isa. 53: 6).

> "I was a wandering sheep,
>   I did not love the fold,
>   I did not love my Shepherd's voice,
>   I would not be controlled:
>   I was a wayward child,
>   I did not love my home,
>   I did not love my Father's voice,
>   I loved afar to roam."

This is what characterizes every man or woman who has never been subdued by divine grace. Sin then is self-will; it is taking my own way and not subjecting myself to the will of God.

The fifth verse tells us, "And ye know that He was manifested to take away our sins; and in Him is no sin." Notice, this is something more than that which is declared in the first chapter of John's Gospel. There John the Baptist exclaims as he points to the Lord Jesus Christ, "Behold the Lamb of God, which taketh away the sin of the world." Here we read, "He was manifested to take away our sins." In the first instance we are directed to the basic work of His cross. There He settled the sin question and because of that finished work He is able to show grace to all men everywhere; but here in the epistle, we have deliverance from the practice of sin, for those who are already saved. "Sin shall not have dominion over you: for ye are not under the law, but under grace." "He was manifested to take away our sins." The Word says, "Thou shalt call His name Jesus: for He shall save His people from their sins" (Matt. 1: 21).

Our blessed Lord not only saves us from the guilt of sin through the work of His cross, but He has provided the means whereby He may save us from the power of sin, take away the habit of sinning, through the indwelling Holy Spirit after the new nature has been communicated to us through the new birth; so that people who loved to sin, loved to take their own way, now delight in holiness and find their joy in doing His will. That is the characteristic mark of a Christian. A man who has professed to accept Christ as his Saviour, to have been justified by faith through His atoning blood, and yet goes on living in the world and like the world, shows that he has never had a renewed nature; is simply a hypocrite, because he is pretending to be what he is not; or else he is self-deceived. But a real Christian is one who has been born again, one who has a new life and a new nature and is indwelt by the Holy Spirit, and therefore, he has learned to hate the sin in which once he lived.

"Ye know that He was manifested to take away our sin; and in Him is no sin." It was said of the sin offering of old, "It is most holy," and so if our blessed Lord Jesus would become the great sin offering here in the world, He must be the Holy One—the Lamb must be without blemish and without spot, outwardly and inwardly. How careful the Spirit of God is to insist that this is ever true of our Lord Jesus Christ. Again and again Scripture dwells upon His infinite beauty and holiness. "He did no sin," and, "In Him is no sin." And now this absolutely sinless One, who in grace became sin for us that we might be reconciled to God, dwells by the Spirit in the believer, and our new nature is really His very life imparted to us. It is in the power of this life that we triumph over sin.

There is a young man in whom I am deeply interested who has been for a long time a confirmed addict to the disgusting cigarette habit. I remember years ago I used to go to restaurants and see signs which read, "Ladies never smoke;

gentlemen must not." Now it seems to be just
the opposite. I used to travel on the Pullman
cars a great deal, and no one ever dreamed of seeing a man smoke in the diner. If one were so
boorish, some railroad official would say, "Excuse
me, sir, but there is no smoking allowed here; go
to the smoker for that." But now I can hardly go
into a diner to eat a meal but I am disgusted by
some painted young woman, sitting perhaps at
the next table, filling the place with the fumes of
tobacco.   Someone said to W. P. Nicholson, the
Irish evangelist, "Can't a real Christian use tobacco?" He answered, "Yes, you dirty beast!
This young man in whom I have been so deeply
interested has tried to free himself from this
habit, he wants to be free, but being of an exceedingly nervous temperament, this thing has
got such a grip on him that unfortunately phys-
icians have told him it would be best to continue
the use of it. I cannot tell you how many times
I have looked at him and said, "Oh, how I wish
it were possible for me in some way to get such
control of your will that this thing would fall off,
because I detest it so! If I could only get within
you so that my mind could control yours, and my
feeling toward this thing take possession of you,
you would never smoke again." And that is exactly what the blessed Lord does for those who
trust Him. He dwells within us, and as we yield
to Him, He takes full control, He dominates the

believer so that he lives to His praise and to His glory. As a silly boy I smoked a few cigarettes, but when I was converted, I was through with it, and it has never been anything but disgusting to me.

Now the apostle goes on to show what holiness really means in the Christian's life. "Whosoever abideth in Him sinneth not (is not characterized by sinning): whosoever sinneth hath not seen Him, neither known Him." That used to trouble me, because I was not clear about it. I used to read it as though it said, "Whosoever committeth a sin hath not seen Him, neither known Him." That eighth verse bothered me particularly: "He that committeth sin is of the devil; for the devil sinneth from the beginning." And as I got my eyes off the Lord and allowed myself to fall into something that dishonored Him, those words were the torment of my life—"He that committeth sin is of the devil." I would say, "I was so sure I was born of God, that I was converted; but has it all been a mistake?" I went to a teacher and asked him about this, and he said, "You have been converted all right, but every time you commit a sin you become unconverted again, and a child of the devil once more." That made me more bewildered than ever, and I thought, "How will I ever know when I am converted to stay; and also if I were converted over and over again, how would I know for sure that I was still converted just before I died? I might suddenly become a child of the devil again and miss everything." That troubled a dear Irishman who had been wonderfully saved, and suddenly the thought came to him, "Dear me, if I am so happy in the Lord now, what an awful thing it would be if something happened that cut me off from Christ and I should be lost after all!" He went to a meeting, and a preacher read these words, "Ye are dead, and your life is hid with Christ in God." It came to that Irish brother with such clarity that he shouted, "Glory to God, whoever heard of a man drowning with his head that high above water!" But here was this plain statement in 1 John 3: 8 before me. I looked back to verse six, and was more bewildered than ever as I read, "Whosoever abideth in Him sinneth not: whosoever sinneth hath not seen Him, neither known Him." They had said to me that even though I might have been a Christian at one time, yet if I sinned, I ceased to be one. But, no; this verse says that whosoever sinneth has never been a Christian at all. I was greatly troubled, for I knew I had not gotten to the place of sinless perfection, but I was trying to get there in those days.

What a relief of mind it was to get a better understanding of the tense of the verbs! Contrast verse one of chapter two, "My little children, these things write I unto you, that ye sin not. And if any man sin, we have an Advocate with the Father, Jesus Christ the righteous." He does not say if any man sin he ceases to be a child of God, but, "We have an Advocate with the Father." The word *sin* is in the aorist tense, and refers to a definite action at a given point of time, "If any man should fall into a sin." But now in the sixth verse, it is the present continuous tense, "Whosoever goes on practising sin, whosoever makes it the habit of his life to live in sin, hath not seen Him, neither known Him." Peter fell into grievous sin, and that sin was repeated and repeated, but when the Lord turned and looked on him, he went out and wept bitterly. His heart was broken because of his failure, and he was soon restored. Real believers fall into sin if their eyes for a moment are taken off the Lord Jesus Christ, but the advocacy of the Lord Jesus begins right there, and He restores their souls.

"Whosoever abideth in Him sinneth not: whosoever sinneth hath not seen Him, neither known Him. Children (this is the word that takes in the whole family of God), let no man deceive you: he that *practiseth* righteousness is righteous, even as *He* is righteous. He that practiseth sin is of the devil; for the devil sinneth (hath made sin a practice) from the beginning." All through his fearful history the devil has been characterized by rebellion against God. He practised sin from the beginning. Those who are children of the devil exhibit the moral characteristics of their father, while those who belong to the family of God exhibit the moral characteristics of their Father. They delight in holiness even as the others roll sin as a sweet morsel under their tongues. For this purpose the Son of God was manifest that He might destroy, undo, annul, the works of the devil. My brother, my sister, there is not only deliverance from the judgment due your sin, but deliverance has been provided from the power of sin, that He might annul the works of the devil, that He might set His people free from the power of sin and Satan, that they might live in this world to the praise of His glory.

"Whosoever is born of God doth not commit sin (practise sin); for his seed remaineth in him: and he cannot sin (cannot be sinning), because he is born of God." When I think of justification, I am thinking of a forensic act of God by which I am cleared of every charge of guilt. When I think of regeneration, I am thinking of the impartation of a new nature in the power of the Holy Spirit by reason of which the whole bent of my life is changed. "Whosoever is born of God doth not commit sin; for his seed remaineth in him: and he cannot sin, because he is born of God."

Years ago when I went to California as a boy, the only oranges we knew were the seedlings. But some years before two of the Washington Navel orange-trees were brought to Riverside from

Brazil and cultivated. Cuttings were taken from these parent trees at Riverside, and orange-trees were budded with the Washington Navel shoots, and their character was completely changed. A man having a forty-acre orchard and not wanting to be left completely without fruit, would have the tops of one-half of the trees cut off, and the other twenty acres would go on bearing the oranges with the seeds. He would cut under the bark of the lopped trees, and put in the Navel orange cuttings, and in a couple of years all those trees would have new branches and would be loaded with oranges. I might say to the owner, "What kind of oranges are these?" "Washington Navel oranges," he would reply. "Is that the only kind of oranges they bear? Don't they sometimes bear seedlings?" "Oh, no," he would say; "A budded tree does not produce seedlings." But even as he is speaking I might stoop down and see a little shoot under the branches coming out of the trunk of the tree, and say, "Look, what is that shoot?" He would snip it off, or taking his knife out of his pocket would cut it away, saying, "That's from below the graft. It must be pruned off." You see what is characteristic of the budded tree is that it bears the Navel oranges, but if one does not watch, below the grafting there will be a shoot of the old nature. And so as children of God we cannot go on living in sin. If you ever find a Christian slipping into anything unclean or unholy, you may know that this comes from below the graft—it is the old nature manifesting itself!

How can you keep the old nature from producing sin? By using the pruning-knife of self-judgment. Whenever you find any tendency of insubjection to God, of self-will, a tendency to think of unclean or unholy things, get out the pruning-knife and use it unsparingly on yourself. This thing is of the old nature, not of the new, and it must not be allowed to grow, to develop, or it will destroy your fellowship with God. "Whosoever is born of God doth not commit sin; for his seed remaineth in him: and he cannot sin, because he is born of God." That new life which has been committed to him is eternal life; it abides in him, and he cannot be sinning because he is born of God.

The tenth verse epitomizes it all: "In this the children of God are manifest, and the children of the devil: whosoever doeth not righteousness is not of God, neither he that loveth not his brother." My dear friend, face the question, face the fact of those two families. Men talk about the universal Fatherhood of God and the brotherhood of man, and would have us believe that all men are looked upon by God as His children. Remember that the tenderest, the holiest Man that ever walked this earth, our blessed Lord Jesus Christ, was the One who taught the very opposite. I cannot understand these men who tell us that Jesus came to teach this very doctrine of the universal Fatherhood of God and the universal brotherhood of man. What did He mean, then, when He said to the Pharisees, "Ye are of your father the devil, and the works of your father ye will do?" What did He mean when He said to Nicodemus, "Except a man be born again, he cannot see the kingdom of God?" (John 3: 3). John walked with the blessed Lord for those three-and-one-half wonderful years, drank in His testimony as perhaps no other did, and was so intimate with Him that he lay on His bosom at that last supper. He wrote his epistle when he was an old man, and gathered up what he had been taught by the Lord and what he had experienced through the years, and said, as it were, "Here are the two families—the family that loves God and delights in righteousness is the family of God. But the family that hates, that harms, that loves sin and iniquity, is the family of the devil." "In this the children of God are manifest, and the children of the devil: whosoever doeth not righteousness is not of God, neither he that loveth not his brother."

Let us challenge our own hearts. Let us face the question fairly in God's presence. Have I been regenerated by grace divine? If really saved, we shall find the answer in verse fourteen: "We know that we have passed from death unto life, because we love the brethren. He that loveth not his brother abideth in death."

Love, the Proof of Divine Life

————

"For this is the message that ye heard from the beginning, that we should love one another. Not as Cain, who
was of that wicked one, and slew his brother. And wherefore slew he him? Because his own works were evil, and
his brother's righteous. Marvel not, my brethren, if the
world hate you. We know that we have passed from death
unto life, because we love the brethren. He that loveth not
his brother abideth in death. Whosoever hateth his brother
is a murderer: and ye know that no murderer hath eternal
life abiding in him. Hereby perceive we the love of God, because He laid down His life for us: and we ought to lay
down our lives for the brethren. But whoso hath this
world's good, and seeth his brother have need, and shutteth
up his bowels of compassion from him, how dwelleth the
love of God in him?" (1 John 3: 11-17).

"This is the message that ye heard from the
beginning, that we should love one another." We
have noticed a number of times that this expression, "From the beginning," is characteristic of
this epistle. In a day when men were trying to
bring in false teachings and seeking to palm them
off on unsuspecting people as Christianity, when
in reality they were but doctrines of demons, the
apostle calls the Christians back to that which
they had been taught from the beginning, either
by our Lord Jesus Christ directly while on earth,

or by His immediate successors, the apostolic band; and prominent, of course, was that which is here emphasized, "This is the message that ye heard from the beginning, that we should love one another."

There are three distinct words used for *love* in the Greek language. One of these is never used in the New Testament; it is the word, *eros*. You are familiar with that word as the name of the Greek god that answered to the Roman Cupid. According to Roman mythology he was the son of Venus, the goddess of sensual love and physical beauty. Among the Greeks they used the name Aphrodite for the goddess, and Eros for her supposed son. This word for love is never used in the New Testament, for it had been so degraded among the Greeks. It would seem that the Holy Spirit of God stood guard over the pages of the New Testament, and said, as it were, "Do not pollute these pages with a word that has become so debased." The other words are *phileo* and *agapeoo*. The first means affection, friendliness, the kind of love that good-natured people feel one for another. That word is frequently used in the New Testament. It is used of God in one place—"After that the kindness and love of God our Saviour toward man appeared, not by works of righteousness which we have done, but according to His mercy He saved us, by the washing of regeneration, and renewing of the Holy

Ghost" (Titus 3: 4, 5). "Love toward man" is just one word in the original; it is really our word *"philanthropy,"*—the philanthropy of God was manifested in sending His Son. Ordinarily, *phileo* is the word that is used for love between friends, brothers, sisters, husband, wife, and sometimes between Christians, but it is not used in the sense that the word *agapeoo* is used. This signifies a love that is Divine.

God is *agape.* He Himself is love in His very essence, and "he that dwelleth in love (in this sense), dwelleth in God." It is love in this high sense, in this divine sense, that is brought before us in this portion of the epistle—love as the proof of a new nature, the evidence that we have been regenerated.

The one great command that is laid upon us by our Lord Jesus is that we love one another, love as He loved us, unselfishly, in a God-like, Christ-like way. "Not as Cain, who was of that wicked one, and slew his brother." Cain was stirred up by jealousy and lured on by envy. "Wherefore slew he him? Because his own works were evil, and his brother's righteous." What a wretched thing is that vile sin of envy or jealousy. Scripture says that jealousy is "cruel as the grave." I pray you, dear children of God, never permit yourselves to harbor that wicked thing. Perhaps God has given you some little ability along some line, but if as you see someone else

who seems to be more appreciated than you, and
there arises within you that abominable jealousy,
check it immediately. Go into the presence of
God at once and confess the sin of it, the wickedness of it, ask Him to so fill you with Himself that
there will be no place for it. I have seen it among
Christian workers, I have felt it in my own heart
in connection with other preachers. One man has
a message from God and he gives it in the power
of the Holy Ghost, and another cannot bear to
think that his brother's message is so much appreciated and so greatly used, and he falls under
the power of the same thing that led Cain to slay
his brother, Abel. I have seen it, also, among
those who sing the gospel. There may be one to
whom God has given a marvelous voice, but instead of carrying out his own service and rejoic-
ing in whatever ability God has given another, he
is torn by envy and rent by jealousy because another is appreciated in place of himself. I have
seen it in the Sewing Circle, in the Sunday School,
and even in work in connection with ministering
to the temporal needs of the saints. I remember
attending a fellowship tea where two good sisters
would not speak to nor look at each other because
one had found that the efforts of the other were
appreciated more than her own. What a wretched
thing this professional jealousy is! There is no
room for it in love, in the new nature; and whenever you find it, it is simply an evidence of an

unchanged old nature; it is a shoot from the old thing that ought to be crucified. In the light of the cross of Christ, we realize as nowhere else that jealousy is indeed as cruel as the grave; and because of this cruel thing, people will tear one another's reputations to pieces and go all lengths in order to belittle and degrade them. It seems so strange that we Christians, hated by the world, just a little flock after all, should ever suffer ourselves to indulge in such unkind feelings toward one another.

The story is told of Nelson, when, as his ships were drawn up in battle-array facing the Dutch fleet, he saw two English officers quarreling. He threw himself in between and pushed them apart, as he said, pointing to the ships of Holland, "Gentlemen, there are your enemies!" Would God that Christians would indeed love one another, then it would not trouble us if the world hated us. "Marvel not, my brethren, if the world hate you. We know that we have passed from death unto life, because we love the brethren. He that loveth not his brother abideth in death." Do we know that we have passed from death unto life because we are so sound in the faith, because we are fundamentalists, because we are such earnest Christian workers, because we give so liberally to missions and to sustain the Lord's work? Oh, no. What, then? "We know that we have passed from death unto life, because we love the breth-

ren." We love them in this divine sense. Oh, my
brethren, my sisters, if you have not that testimony you had better begin to investigate the
foundations of the house of your Christian profession. "We know that we have passed from death
unto life, because we love the brethren." Some of
us in our unconverted days did not love them very
much. I remember when some of them would
come to our home when I was a boy. They were
stern old Scotchmen, and would say, "Harry, lad,
are ye born again yet?" And I wouldna ken what
to say. How I detested them! And then one day
God came in in grace and saved my soul, and I
could hardly wait to get down to see some of them
and say, "Thank God, I am saved!" It makes
such a difference; for this being born again, this
being converted to God, is a real thing. It is the
impartation of a new nature, a divine nature, the
very essence of which is love.

By this "we know that we have passed from
death unto life, because we love the brethren. He
that loveth not his brother abideth in death. Whosoever hateth his brother is a murderer: and ye
know that no murderer hath eternal life abiding
in him." The same thing that produces the sin
of murder is that which leads you to hate your
brother. It may not yet have gone just that far.
I heard a professed Christian woman speaking of
another, and between her clenched teeth, she said,
"I wish she were dead." What is that? That is

murder; that is the thing that sends men to the gallows and to the electric chair. "Whosoever hateth his brother is a murderer: and ye know that no murderer hath eternal life abiding in him." "But," you say, "you heard a *Christian* woman say that?" Yes, but that was just for a moment, when she allowed the old nature to assert itself. She soon judged it and put it away. If Christians get out of touch with God, there may be a manifestation of that old thing, the flesh, or carnal mind; but they are indwelt by the Holy Ghost, and He will soon make them intensely miserable, and they will judge it and put it in the place of death. But no one who wilfully goes on in these things has any business calling himself a child of God. No one who is characterized by hatred has eternal life abiding in him. No murderer possesses this blessing, and hatred is the root of murder.

This does not mean that an actual murderer cannot be saved, but it does mean that if he is saved, he will no longer live in hatred. "Hereby perceive we the love of God, because He laid down His life for us: and we ought to lay down our lives for the brethren." You will observe that the words "of God" are italicized. John is not exactly saying, "Hereby perceive we the love of God," but he has been telling us that as Christians we should love one another, and if we want to understand what love is, he gives us a sample—hereby we recognize what love is because, "He laid down His life for us: and we ought to lay down our lives for the brethren." It is not exactly, herein is *God's love* manifested but, if you ask what is meant by such love, this is the example. As a Christian, that which is manifested in Christ must be manifested in you. You must be willing to lay down your life for others, to endure any kind of hardship in order that you may help and bless others.

Years ago when I was a Salvation Army officer, the General, William Booth, was over in London, an old man and blind. They had hoped to have him present at a great Congress, but word was sent that he could not come. Then they asked for a letter from him, some message to read to the assembled officers, but no letter came. By and by when the Congress was in session, a boy came up the aisle with an envelope. It was given to the officer in charge, and as he held it up he said, "A message from General Booth!" He opened it, and said, "My comrades, it contains just one word —'Others.'" That was all. That was what the old man had lived for, and that was what he would impress upon those who followed him. After all, that is the only happy life. The most miserable people are those who are trying to get the best for themselves, while the happiest people are those who give the most, sacrifice the most, and lay themselves out the most for the blessing

of others. There is real joy in laying down one's
life for the brethren. There are always those
who will say, "But really, you are working too
hard; you ought not to do this, and ought not to
do that." The devil always has a lot of lieutenants
to say, "Do be careful; your health is of so much
importance." It is ten thousand times better to
wear out for Jesus' sake in blessing others, and
hear a "Well done, good and faithful servant,"
than to have to go to the judgment-seat of Christ
and give account of a lifetime of selfishness.

John says, "But whoso hath this world's good,
and seeth his brother have need, and shutteth up
his bowels of compassion from him, how dwelleth
the love of God in him?" Do you say, "I know he
has need, but if he had saved his money as I have
done, he wouldn't be in such a fix; I know his
clothes are shabby, but if he would take care of
them as I do of mine, he wouldn't look like that?"
We read in James 2: 16 of those who say to the
needy, "Depart in peace, be ye warmed and filled,
notwithstanding ye give them not those things
which are needful to the body; what doth it
profit?" And He that is higher than the highest
is looking down and taking note of it all, and
some day the one who turns down God's poor is
going to be poor himself. Perhaps not poor finan-
cially in the same way that the other was, but a
time of great need will come, and he will go to
God and begin to call upon Him in that hour of

distress and wonder that the heavens seem brass above him.

"My little children, let us not love in word, neither in tongue; but in deed and in truth. And hereby we know that we are of the truth, and shall assure our hearts before Him. For if our heart condemn us, God is greater than our heart, and knoweth all things. Beloved, if our heart condemn us not, then have we confidence toward God." If in the secret of our own room in the presence of God, conscience says, "You know you were selfish, you were not considerate, you did not act in love, you did not manifest the Spirit of Christ," remember that "if our heart condemn us, God is greater than our heart, and knoweth all things." Then we read, "Beloved, if our heart condemn us not, then have we confidence toward God. And whatsoever we ask, we receive of Him, because we keep His commandments, and do those things that are pleasing in His sight." Do you get the inference? When you do not receive from Him, it is time to ask, "Have I a condemning heart? My own need is great, and God does not seem to minister to it. Have others come to me in their need, and have I failed to minister to them? I have cried unto God in the depths of my grief and sorrow, but He does not seem to listen. Did any ever cry to me in their grief and sorrow, and did I refuse to listen?" "Whatsoever a man soweth, that shall he also reap." You see,

Christianity is intensely practical, and we have been trying to make it a theoretical thing, and we say, "Is it not true that all who believe on the Lord Jesus Christ shall be saved?" Yes, it is; but you know real faith worketh by love. Do not forget that. We have gone to Him in prayer and there has been no answer, but the secret of our unanswered prayer was in our own heart. We have been so selfish and indifferent to the needs of our brethren. "And this is His commandment, That we should believe on the name of His Son Jesus Christ, and love one another, as He gave us commandment. And he that keepeth His commandments dwelleth in Him, and He in him. And hereby we know that He abideth in us, by the Spirit which He hath given us." That Holy Spirit is the Spirit of love and of power and of a sound mind, and when He dwells within the believer and controls him, that believer walks in love and manifests the kindness of God to his brethren.

Jesus Christ Come in the Flesh

"Beloved, believe not every spirit, but try the spirits whether they are of God: because many false prophets are gone out into the world. Hereby know ye the Spirit of God: Every spirit that confesseth that Jesus Christ is come in the flesh is of God: and every spirit that confesseth not that Jesus Christ is come in the flesh is not of God: and this is that spirit of antichrist, whereof ye have heard that it should come; and even now already is it in the world. Ye are of God, little children, and have overcome them: because greater is He that is in you, than he that is in the world. They are of the world: therefore speak they of the world, and the world heareth them. We are of God: he that knoweth God heareth us; he that is not of God heareth not us. Hereby know we the spirit of truth, and the spirit of error" (1 John 4: 1-6).

"Beloved, believe not every spirit, but try the spirits whether they are of God: because many false prophets are gone out into the world." The Holy Scriptures recognize the fact that there is an unseen spirit-world, and that in that world there are spirits both good and evil. Of the elect angels it is written, He "maketh His angels spirits, and His ministers a flame of fire" (Heb. 1:7). That these spirits have a certain ministry to the people of God here on earth is perfectly clear, for we read, "Are they not all ministering spirits, sent forth to minister for them who shall be heirs of salvation?" (Heb. 1: 14). Their ministry has to do with temporal mercies rather than with the unfolding of spiritual truths, for there is another Spirit greater than all created spirits, to whom it is given to guide us into all truth, that is the Holy Spirit of God, and we as believers look not to the angels for guidance and understanding, but to the Comforter, the Holy Spirit, the divine Person who came into the world to take of the things of Christ and open them to us.

On the other hand, there is a realm of evil spirits. We are told in Ephesians 6: 12 that "we wrestle not against flesh and blood, but against principalities, against powers, against the rulers of the darkness of this world, against spiritual wickedness in high places." It is possible for a man to be under the control of the Holy Spirit to such an extent that He is free to use that man to spread the truth of God in a mighty way, but it is just as possible for a man to be under the control of the evil spirits, and teach lies instead of truth. When under their control he will seek to turn people away from the revealed message that God has given in His Word, and bring them into bondage to some form of error. It is important, therefore, that we should be able to distinguish between the spirit of truth and the spirit of error.

In the early days of the Christian Church there

were those who came in among the assemblies,
professing to be speaking by the Spirit of God,
but teaching something contrary to what was
plainly declared in the Word of God, and so John
wrote, "Believe not every spirit, but try (or test)
the spirits whether they are of God." But how
may we test them? Inquire whether their utterances are in accordance with what is revealed
in this Book, for this was given by inspiration of
God. "Holy men of God spake as they were
moved by the Holy Ghost" (2 Pet. 1: 21). Therefore, no man speaking by the Spirit will give
utterance to anything that contradicts that revelation.

We have here that which is of tremendous importance in our day as well as in John's day, for
there are still multitudes who profess to interpret
the message of God to man, and claim to be under
the controlling power of the divine Spirit, who
in reality are controlled by evil spirits, by demon
powers, speaking things that they ought not to
speak. Scripture says that for filthy lucre's sake
many false prophets are gone out into the world.
A prophet is not necessarily one who foretells the
future, but is one who comes to man with a message from God. "He that prophesieth speaketh
unto men to edification, and exhortation, and comfort" (1 Cor. 14: 3). So, when one comes professing to be a messenger from God, he must be
tested by the Word.

The test is in the second verse, "Hereby know ye the Spirit of God: Every spirit that confesseth that Jesus Christ is come in the flesh is of God." And then in the next verse, contrariwise, "And every spirit that confesseth not that Jesus Christ is come in the flesh is not of God: and this is that spirit of antichrist, whereof ye have heard that it should come; and even now already is it in the world." Notice the simplicity of this. Does a man confess that Jesus Christ is come in the flesh, or does he deny the great doctrine of the incarnation? If a man confesses the incarnation, he is of God. That does not mean that everything else he teaches is necessarily scriptural, but he has the right foundation if he confesses the incarnation of our Lord Jesus Christ.

We begin—the whole Christian system begins—with the incarnation, not with an *apotheosis*. I do not like to use this theological term, for some of you may be asking, "What does it mean?" But it is such a convenient term, and stands in such direct contrast to the other term which we do understand. The word *apotheosis* comes from two Greek words, one meaning *from,* and the other *God* or the *Deity*. So we speak of an apotheosis as a man entirely under an influence from God;— a deified man. There are many ministers and instructors to-day who teach that in our Lord Jesus Christ we have a remarkable youth, a child born into this world in many respects the superior of any other child, a religious genius, who from buding consciousness was God-intoxicated, the bent of whose whole mind was toward a greater knowledge of the Deity, who was always reaching out after God, was so constantly under His influence and so absorbed in Him that He eventually became like Him, and therefore, we see in Jesus Christ, God manifested. That is an apotheosis, that is what is commonly taught by those who are called "Modernists." They deny the incarnation, they affirm an apotheosis. The Word of God does not teach an apotheosis, but it does teach the incarnation.

What do we mean by the incarnation? We mean that God, who existed from eternity in three Persons, Father, Son, and Holy Spirit, desiring to make Himself known to men, to take upon Himself man's sin and iniquity, and to make full atonement for them, stooped in grace in the Person of the Son to identify Himself with humanity, and became incarnate by taking upon Himself flesh and blood. But, remember, it was God who did that. The Babe in Bethlehem was not merely a remarkable child who was born with a great religious instinct, but that Babe was God the Son, who stooped in grace to tenant the virgin's womb, and was born into this world as man, but did not cease for one moment to be God. "Every spirit that confesseth that Jesus Christ is come in the flesh, is of God." Not that Jesus Christ began to be when He was born into the world, but that He *came*—came from where? From heaven. Every spirit that confesseth this is of God. This is the incarnation. Did you ever stop to think what a remarkable expression this is, "Jesus Christ came?" You were *born* into the world; you had no existence before you were born. Poetically, we ask,

"Where did you come from, baby dear?"

and the answer comes,

"Out of the everywhere into here."

"Where did you get those eyes so blue?
They came from the sky as I came through."

But they didn't, you know, that is only poetry. You *began* here on earth; you came into existence when you were born of your parents. But that blessed One did not begin to be when He was born in the stable and cradled in the manger; He came from heaven's highest glory down into this world to be the Saviour of the world. He who was higher than all of the angels, He, their Creator, became a little lower than these glorious beings in order that He, by the grace of God, might taste death for every man. Men may profess to honor Him while teaching an apotheosis, profess to think a great deal of Him by speaking of Him as the greatest religious genius that the world has ever known, may go even as far as the French infidel, Renan, who declared, "From henceforth shall no man distinguish between Thee and God," but that only means that He, a man, has become so god-like that we see God manifested in Him. That is not the incarnation. The great truth is that "God was in Christ, reconciling the world unto Himself, not imputing their trespasses unto them; and hath committed unto us the word of reconciliation" (2 Cor. 5: 19). "Great is the mystery of godliness: God was manifest in the flesh, justified in the Spirit, seen of angels, preached unto the Gentiles, believed on in the world, received up into glory" (1 Tim. 3: 16). This is the Christian confession. Men may profess to honor Jesus while recognizing Him as the mightiest among the mighty, the greatest of all the great men of the world, the most marvelous of all its ethical teachers, but in reality they are but degrading Him unless they acknowledge Him as God over all, God blessed forever, Jesus the Anointed, come in the flesh.

The denial of this then is the spirit of antichrist; and, notice, this denial may be couched in rude or ignorant terms, or it may be presented in beautiful language, but it is the same thing. To think of Jesus as any one else than God, the Creator become Man for our redemption, is to deny the truth concerning Him revealed in this Book, and is the spirit of the antichrist.

Turning to believers with a word of warning, the apostle says, "Ye are of God, little children, and have overcome them: because greater is He that is in you, than he that is in the world." What does he mean by that? Simply this; none of us would be what we are apart from the inworking of the blessed Holy Spirit. The difference between the believer in the Deity of our Lord Jesus Christ and an unbeliever in this great truth, is not as though two men were sitting on a fence and there came an earthquake, and one tumbled backward and another forward, and neither are to blame—one man by chance a Trinitarian, another a Unitarian; one happens to believe that Jesus is God, and one happens to deny it. Not at all! No man would ever acknowledge Him as God become flesh except by the illumination of the Holy Ghost, and even though men acknowledge that only intellectually, it is because God has illumined the mind. But when men bow at the feet of the Saviour and own Him as their Lord and Redeemer, that is the work of the Holy Spirit of God winning their hearts for Himself; and from that moment on it is He who dwells in them, who leads them on into fuller and clearer light and enables them to overcome, and so the believer takes no credit to himself, but gives all the glory to God, for thus illuminating him and saving his soul.

My responsibility begins here. The Spirit of

God illumines the mind and exercises the conscience, and I follow on in accordance with His leading, until I am brought to a full acceptance and acknowledgement of Jesus Christ as Saviour and Lord. The man who thus follows the leading of the Holy Spirit of God must see in Jesus Christ, God the Son become Man for our redemption. It is to such he says, "Ye are of God." You know, when we speak of believing on the Lord Jesus Christ, we mean a great deal more than simply accepting a dogma regarding Jesus Christ as God. I owe all the allegiance of my heart and life to God, my Creator, and if I acknowledge Jesus Christ as God, I owe the allegiance of my heart and life to Him, and when I have been led by the Spirit of God to so put my trust in Him that makes me a Christian.

To believe in Him is to trust Him. You might stand by the side of the sea looking upon a great ship lying at anchor, and say, "I believe that is a splendid ship; I believe that it is thoroughly seaworthy; I believe that it is properly manned; I believe it would take me to yonder distant shore to which I journey." You may believe all that, but if you do not step aboard that ship it will never take you there. And so intellectually you may believe what is recorded about Jesus Christ, you may accept the full scriptural declaration about Him, but unless you trust yourself to Him, He will never be your Saviour and Redeemer.

When you trust Him, you come into this family
of which John is writing, and are one of God's
children, and so it can be said of you, "Ye are
of God, little children." When you turn away
from the world and walk in obedience to His
Word, you are a member of His family, not
through any power of your own, but through the
indwelling Holy Spirit, for, "Greater is He that
is in you, than he that is in the world."

Those who deny the Deity of our blessed Lord
are of the world. They will always be the popular
ones down here, "And the world heareth them."
Of course the world will always ridicule the man
who stakes everything for eternity upon a divine
revelation, and it will honor the man who says,
"I do not accept anything from God; I depend
entirely upon my own sound judgment." It can
understand that kind of talk, for the wisdom of
God is foolishness to the worldly-wise, but "it
pleased God by the foolishness of preaching (not,
through foolish preaching) to save them that believe" (1 Cor. 1: 21). The world does not understand that, but those who are born of God have
an understanding far beyond that of earth. They
who deny the truth are of the world, "therefore
speak they of the world, and the world heareth
them." It is not egotism that leads John to say,
"We are of God." It was the confession that
he and his fellow-apostles (for he speaks for them
as representing the apostolic company when he

uses this language) had the privilege of having
walked for three-and-one-half wonderful years
here on earth with One whom they knew must be
more than man.   Of Him John said, "The Word
became flesh, and *tabernacled* among us (and we
beheld His glory, the glory as of the only begotten
of the Father), full of grace and truth" (John 1:
14).   Knowing Him so intimately, John had in-
dubitable proof that He was more than man.   And
when He died, and came forth in triumph from
the tomb, and they met Him on resurrection
ground, their faith was again confirmed.   Then,
later, when the Holy Spirit descended at Pentecost
and brought them the message that the risen
Christ was exalted to God's right hand, and em-
powered them to go forth and preach the gospel,
there was no doubt left, the last vestige of unbelief disappeared, and they could say, "We know
that we are of God."

"He that knoweth God, heareth us; he that is
not of God, heareth not us.   Hereby know we the
spirit of truth, and the spirit of error."   Any
man who knows God will hear the Word of God.
We can test ourselves by that.   Do you accept the
testimony given in this blessed Word, the testimony of our Lord Himself?   He that is of God
hears this testimony, and he that is not of God
rejects it, and John says, "Hereby know we the
spirit of truth, and the spirit of error."   What
a blessed thing it is to know God as revealed in

the Lord Jesus Christ.   What a wonderful thing
it is to realize that He has come so close to us.
He, the infinite holy One whom these poor finite
minds of ours could not comprehend, has become
Man, that we might see in Him God fully revealed.   Shall we not praise Him and adore Him?

Life and Propitiation in Christ

"Beloved, let us love one another: for love is of God; and every one that loveth is born of God, and knoweth God. He that loveth not, knoweth not God: for God is love. In this was manifested the love of God toward us, because that God sent His only begotten Son into the world, that we might live through Him. Herein is love, not that we loved God, but that He loved us, and sent His Son to be the propitiation for our sins" (1 John 4: 7-10).

Notice that after the parenthesis of verses 1 to 6 in which believers are warned against the false teachers and the evil spirits that have gone out into the world, and are seeking to turn the hearts of God's people away from Christ, the apostle returns to the theme of which he had previously written, the love which is the manifestation of the divine nature.

Let me remind you again that one of the words for *love* used in the New Testament, is that of mere human affection, although it is used also when God is spoken of as being a Friend to man. The other word speaks of a more utterly unselfish affection, a love which is seen in all its fulness in God Himself, and which was manifested in our Lord Jesus Christ when here below, and so when the apostle says, "Beloved, let us love one another," he does not merely seek to inculcate a natural affection, but has in mind the divine affec-

tion wrought in our souls by the Holy Ghost. The
love of God is shed abroad in our hearts by the
Holy Spirit; it is given unto us by Him. Being
possessed of a new and divine nature, having been
regenerated, the natural thing for the believer in
the Lord Jesus is to love. "Let us love one another: for love is of God," in the sense that it is
simply the manifestation of that divine nature
which He has implanted within us. If you find
a person who is not characterized by divine love,
bearing the name of Christian, you may be reason-
ably sure that such an one has never yet been
born again. On the other hand, be careful about
snap judgments lest you yourself fail to manifest
divine love.

"Every one that loveth is born of God, and
knoweth God." Not merely everyone who has
natural affection, who loves father or mother or
children or sister or brother on the human plane,
but every one who loves in this divine unselfish
way, manifests thereby the fact that he is born
of God. Have you been born of God? I am
afraid that people get in the habit of attending
services and of listening to Bible expositions, and
in a measure perhaps they even enjoy them, yet
the power of them never grips their own souls.
Let us never forget the solemn words of our
Lord Jesus Christ, "Ye must be born again."
We are told that John Wesley used to ring
the changes on that text over and over again,

until some people grew weary of hearing it and wished that he would use another theme. One time after having preached on it in a place where he had often done the same before, some one said, "Mr. Wesley, why do you preach so often on that one text, 'Ye must be born again?'" "Why?" exclaimed Mr. Wesley; "Because 'Ye must be born again.'" That is the great thing that is lacking to-day. People imagine they must join the church, be benevolent, turn over a new leaf, be good citizens, be one hundred per cent American—and all these things, they think, constitute Christianity. But, my dear friend, you can do and be all these things and yet be lost for all eternity, for, "Except a man be born again, he cannot see the kingdom of God." The proof that one has been born again is that he manifests this divine love. "Every one that loveth is born of God, and knoweth God," and contrariwise, "He that loveth not, knoweth not God; for God is love."

Twice in this chapter we have that wonderful statement, "God is love." Nowhere else in the world will you find it except in this blessed Book and in other books that have drawn from it.

Years ago a lady who prided herself on belonging to the intelligentsia said to me, "I have no use for the Bible, for Christian superstition, and religious dogma. It is enough for me to know that God is love. "Well," I said, "do you know it?" "Why, of course I do," she said; "we all

know that, and that is religion enough for me. I
do not need the dogmas of the Bible." "How did
you find out that God is love?" I asked. "Why,"
she said, "everybody knows that." "Do they
know it yonder in India?" I asked. "That poor
mother in her distress throwing her little babe
into the holy Ganges to be eaten by filthy and
repulsive crocodiles as a sacrifice for her sins—
does she know that God is love?" "Oh, well, she
is ignorant and superstitious," she replied. "Those
poor wretched negroes in the jungles of Africa,
bowing down to gods of wood and stone, and in
constant fear of their fetishes, the poor heathen
in other countries, do they know that God is love?"
"Perhaps not," she said, "but in a civilized land
we all know it." "But how is it that we know it?
Who told us so? Where did we find it out?" "I do
not understand what you mean," she said, "for
I've always known it." "Let me tell you this," I
answered; "no one in the world ever knew it until
it was revealed from heaven and recorded in the
Word of God. It is here and nowhere else. It is
not found in all the literature of the ancients."

How has that love been manifested? That is
what the apostle shows us in the next two verses.
"God is love"—this is the divine nature. God is
gracious, but it would not do to say that God is
grace; God is merciful, but I could not properly
say that God is mercy; God is kind, but I cannot
say that God is kindness; God is just, but I can-

not say that God is justice, but I can say, because Scripture says so, that God is love. This is the divine nature, the very nature of God, and twice over you get it in this epistle.

If some one said to you, "Where is that text, 'God is love?'" would you remember that it is in the first epistle of John, and could you tell them where to locate it? Let me give you a child's simple arithmetical problem. Twice four is eight, and twice eight is sixteen, and "God is love" is found in 1 John 4:8 and 16. That is where you learn that "God is love." And so we find in this the manifestation of the love of God, "because that God sent His only begotten Son into the world, that we might live through Him." That is the first manifestation of divine love. Creation told out God's omnipotent power and wisdom, but creation could not tell out His love. But when God looked down upon a world of men groaning under the sentence of death because of sin, a world of men who were alive to the things of this life, but utterly dead toward the things of God, dead in trespasses and sins, God found it in His heart to go down after those men and find a means of quickening whosoever will into newness of life. He said, "I am going to give them the greatest Gift that one could possibly give, My only begotten Son. I am going to send Him into that world that they may have life through Him." "In this was manifested the love of God toward us, because that God sent His only begotten Son into the world, that we might live through Him."

Five times in the New Testament you will find the expression,"The Only Begotten," and it always speaks of what our blessed Lord is in His eternal relationship to the Father—the Eternal Son, the Only Begotten. It does not speak of any thought of priority on the part of the Father. There is no thought of generation connected with it. You will see that when you notice how the same word is used in Hebrews 11. There you read of Abraham who had received the promise and offered up his *only begotten son*. Now notice, Isaac was not his only son. By natural generation, Abraham was the father of Ishmael years before Isaac was born, but Isaac is called his only begotten son. Why? Because Isaac was his son by a miraculous, unique relationship in which no other son could ever share. He had other sons afterwards, through Keturah, but none had the same relationship to him that Isaac had. And so this term "The Only Begotten Son," tells of our blessed Lord in the past eternity as one Person of the adorable Trinity in eternal relation with the Father. It might be translated His *unique Son*. Others are sons by creation, as Adam was, and as angels are, or by new birth, as believers are, but He alone is the unique Son.

Five times He is called "The Only Begotten," and five times "The First Begotten." In the lat-

ter term you have a different thought altogether.
You have Him coming into the world, going down
into death, and rising in triumph at the head of
a new creation, and thus He is the First Begotten, through whom God is bringing many sons
into glory, and by and by the many sons will shine
resplendent in the same glory, but not one of us
will enter into the relation of the only begotten
Son. That remains unique for all eternity. Think
of it! God, the Father, loved a world dead in
trespasses and sins in such a way that He gave
His unique Son, the darling of His bosom, that
we might live unto Him.

Because we were dead we needed life, and there
is no life apart from Him. "He that hath the Son
hath life; and he that hath not the Son hath not
life." No works, no efforts of ours, could ever
produce divine life. You could not make yourself
become a Christian, a child of God; you could not
by any effort of your own, by any prayers, any
penances, produce one spark of divine life within
your soul. But the moment you receive Christ,
you have received Him who is the life. "God so
loved the world, that He gave His only begotten
Son, that whosoever believeth in Him, should not
perish, but have everlasting life."

> "Life is found alone in Jesus,
> Only there 'tis offered thee—
> Offered without price or money,
> 'Tis the gift of God sent free.
> Take salvation—
> Take it now, and happy be."

While it is true that as dead sinners we need
life, there is something required in order that
God may righteously accept us in a position of
perfect justification in His sight.   There was a
work that had to be done that we could never do;
and that, God in His infinite love and grace, sent
His Son to accomplish.   The second great proof of
His love is found in verse 10, "Herein is love, not
that we loved God, but that He loved us, and sent
His Son to be the propitiation for our sins."   It
is God who came out to us; we did not seek after
Him.   For, alas, we did not love God; our hearts
were filled with enmity against Him.   But He met
our every need.   You see, because we were dead
we needed life, and God sent Christ that we might
live through Him.   Because we were sinners lost
and guilty it was necessary that a propitiation be
made for sin, and God sent His Son to effect that
propitiation.

It is an interesting fact that the original word
translated *propitiation* is exactly the same word
that is used for "atonement" in the Septuagint
translation of the Old Testament, a Greek translation made from the Hebrew around 230 B. C.,
by a group of scholars in Alexandria, Egypt.   In
that translation of the Old Testament wherever
the translators sought to reproduce the Hebrew
word *caphar,* or *atonement,* they used the Greek
word here rendered *propitiation.*   The Hebrew
word *atonement* comes from a root meaning *to*

cover, and so this word speaks of an expiation, a settling of the sin-question, so that one who was once lost and guilty may stand in the presence of God without one charge against him. All his transgressions are covered by the finished work of the Lord Jesus Christ;—covered so effectually and completely that they will never be found again.

> " Clean ev'ry whit;' Thou saidst it, Lord;
>   Shall one suspicion lurk?
>   Thine surely is a faithful Word,
>   And Thine a finished work."

There yonder on the cross the blessed Son of God took our place in judgment. But it was not merely the sufferings that men heaped upon Jesus that settled the sin-question; but there as He hung upon the cross when that supernatural darkness covered all the scene, we read, "Jehovah made His soul an offering for sin." In those hours of darkness God was dealing with His Son about that awful question, and there He bore in His inmost soul the judgment that you and I would have to bear ourselves for all eternity if left without a Saviour. Thus He became the propitiation, the expiation for our sins, and in this we see manifested to the fullest extent the love of God.

"Herein is love, not that we loved God, but that He loved us, and sent His Son to be the propitiation for our sins." This indeed is love. We hated Him, we loved our own way, we wanted to take our own course, we did not want to be submissive to His holy will, but He loved us and looked upon us in grace, He yearned to have us with Him in glory free from every stain of sin, and because there was no other way whereby that could be effected, He sent His Son to become the propitiation for our sins.   Do not talk about believing that God is love if you do not accept the gift of His love, the Lord Jesus Christ, for in Him alone we have life and propitiation.   "There is none other name under heaven given among men, whereby we must be saved," but the name of our Lord Jesus Christ.

God Manifested in Love

"Beloved, if God so loved us, we ought also to love one another. No man hath seen God at any time. If we love one another, God dwelleth in us, and His love is perfected in us. Hereby know we that we dwell in Him, and He in us, because He hath given us of His Spirit" (1 John 4:11 —13).

Notice carefully what the Spirit of God brings before us here. First, "Beloved, if God so loved us." What does He mean when He puts in this little word *so?* It carries our minds back to the tenth verse, "Herein is love, not that we loved God, but that He loved us, and sent His Son to be the propitiation for our sins." That is the way God *so* loved us. He did not wait for us to love Him before loving us; He did not wait for us to behave ourselves so well that He could look upon us with complacency, but "God commendeth His love toward us, in that, while we were yet sinners, Christ died for us" (Rom. 5:8). God loved us when there was nothing lovable about us, God loved us when we were in enmity against Him and "alienated by wicked works," God loved us when our desires were contrary to His desires, when we were trampling His Word beneath our feet, spurning His grace, breaking His commandments; and now we read, "Beloved, if God so loved us, we ought also to love one another."

We remember the words of our Lord Jesus Christ, "If ye love them which love you, what reward have ye? Do not even the publicans the same?" Why, the most wretched creatures in the world love those out of whom they get some satisfaction, those who seem to give them some return for their affection, but the great principle laid down here is that after we have been born of God and are partakers of the divine nature, we will not wait for people to love us, to behave themselves in a way satisfactory to us, but however they behave themselves we will go on loving them just the same. That is divine love manifested through the new nature. That is a challenge even to Christians, because we still have the old nature in us. Though born of God, the Christian has a nature that came from fallen Adam, and that nature is selfish and is looking for satisfaction in others and in the things of this world. It is only through the power of the new nature, the divine nature, communicated by the second birth, that the Christian can rise to the standard set before him.

"Beloved, if God so loved us, we ought also to love one another." I like that word, *ought*. It suggests duty. Sometimes Christians do not like to be reminded of duty, for they have an idea that duty is not consistent with grace. But the grace of God, when it is active in the life, leads men and women to do the things they ought to do.

Here is one thing we ought to do, we ought to love one another; we ought to love those that do not love us, those who mistreat us, those who speak evil of us, those who harm us, those who would ruin us if they could. That is the way God loves us. Nothing that men did to our blessed Lord Jesus, nothing that they said about Him, could change the attitude of His heart toward them. As He was hanging extended upon the cross of shame, and that angry rabble cried out for His life, He prayed, "Father, forgive them; for they know not what they do!" (Luke 23:34). This is not natural. No man will love like this naturally. But this is spiritual, this is divine, and this is possible as we walk in the power of the new nature which God has communicated to those who believe.

Then observe verse 12, "No man hath seen God at any time." This is not the first time that this expression is found in the Scriptures. Turn to John 1:18, and you will find exactly the same words, "No man hath seen God at any time." Let us consider these words which are sometimes called in question. People say, "Do we not read of many instances in Scripture where men saw God? Did not God speak with Moses face to face, and did He not put him in a cleft of the rock while He passed by? Did not Adam speak with God in the garden? Do we not read in Isaiah 6:1, 'In the year that king Uzziah died, I saw also the

Lord sitting upon a throne, high and lifted up, and His train filled the temple?' Did not Ezekiel have visions of God, and did not the glory of the Lord appear to Daniel and to many another?" Yes, undoubtedly; and yet it remains true that, "No man hath seen God at any time." For God is a Spirit, infinite, eternal, and is Himself invisible. However, Christ has made God manifest to men. But before He became incarnate, God the Father, God the Son, and God the Spirit were alike invisible. Those of whom it is written that they saw God, saw some form which God took, a Theophany, by which He manifested Himself unto them. They saw His glory, the outshining of His splendor, but they could not see Deity as such.

No one, in a sense, has ever seen you. People have seen your body, your face, your eyes, but they have never seen you, they have never seen the spirit that looks out through those eyes. We cannot see the real man, for under present conditions the spirit of man is invisible. We shall never really see one another as long as we are in the flesh; but by and by we shall see and know one another in spirit but not while we are here in the body. No one has ever seen the sun. Somebody might object to that and say, "Why, how can you tell me that I have never seen the sun! Of course I have seen it. I have seen it rise, I have seen it moving through the heavens in splendor,

I have seen it set as it drops into the west." But
you are mistaken. You have never seen the sun!
You have seen the robe of glory that envelopes
it, but you cannot pierce that glory and see behind the flame that enfolds that great globe. That
would be impossible. It is the sun that gives out
that glory and you cannot even gaze upon that
in its full strength at noonday for one minute,
because of its blinding glare. A great astronomer
was so delighted when one of the finest telescopes
was first invented, that in his haste to look at
the sun through it, he forgot to put the dark glass
over the lens, and swinging that great instrument
into place, he leaned down and with the naked
eye looked through the lens at the sun. The next
moment he uttered a cry of pain as the blinding
light burned his eye, destroying its sight completely.

Plato said, "The radiant light is the shadow of
God." David declared of God, "Thou clothest
Thyself with light as with a garment." There
you have it—the light, the glory, the radiance is
just the garment, and God is behind it all, invisible.

We read in John 1: 18 that "the only begotten
Son, subsisting in the bosom of the Father, hath
declared Him"— made Him manifest. That is,
our blessed Lord Jesus Christ coming into the
world as God manifest in the flesh has now made
God known to man. We understand Him as we

could not have done otherwise. Jesus says, "He that hath seen Me hath seen the Father."

In Hebrews we read that He is the express image of the Father. The real meaning of this is that He is the exact expression of His character. All that God is, is told out in Jesus. Jesus walked this world for a brief period of thirty-three and one-half years, and during that time God was manifest, God was seen on the earth, in the person of His blessed Son. And when He went back to heaven from which He came, was God left without any manifestation down here? We read, "No man hath seen God at any time. If we love one another, God abideth in us, and His love is perfected in us." It is not merely that God dwells in us, for God dwells in all believers, but the Greek word for *dwelleth* is different from that for *abideth*. If we love one another, we manifest the new and divine nature; if we walk in love, then men can see God in us, for God *abideth* in us. That is, if we are living in fellowship with God, we are manifesting God, making God known.

We all noticed a short time ago the account of the professed conversion of the President of China. We hope there has been a real work in his soul, but time will tell. I was reading how he came to his Christian wife who was saved long before he made a profession, and said, "I can't understand these Christians; why, they have been treated most abominably here, they have been robbed, beaten, many of them killed, they have been persecuted fearfully, and yet I never find one of them retaliating, and any time they can do anything for China, for our people, they are ready to do it; I do not understand them." "Well," said his wife, "that, you see, is the very essence of Christianity. They do that because they are Christians." That is how God is manifest, is seen, yonder in China, and that is how you and I are called upon to manifest God wherever we may be. Many men will not even read His Word, but they are reading us, they are looking at our lives. How much of God is really seen in us? You know that little verse:

"You are writing a Gospel, a chapter a day,
 By deeds that you do, by words that you say.
 Men read what you write, whether faithless or true;
 Say, what is the Gospel *according to you?*"

A great many men never read the Gospel according to Matthew, they never put in any time on the Gospel according to Luke, they never look into the Gospel according to Mark, never weigh the Gospel according to John, but they are reading the Gospel according to you, and weighing you; they are watching you, listening to what you say, observing what you do, and getting their ideas of Christ and their ideas of God from what they see in you.

A number of years ago I was down in Ganado, Arizona, visiting the Presbyterian Mission. In the hospital there was a poor Navajo woman who had been in a most desperate condition but had been nursed back to life and health through the Christian missionary doctor and the consecrated nurses. She was a poor heathen woman and had had a most dreadful experience. She had been cast out by her own people when they thought she was going to die, and had been thrown behind a clump of brush and left there for three or four days in mid-August, when the heat is terrific during the day time and the nights become bitterly cold. There she lay without food or drink, suffering dreadfully. This missionary doctor found her there, brought her to the hospital, and did everything that Christian love and surgical skill could suggest, and at last brought her back to health. After nine weeks in the hospital, she began to wonder about everything, and said to the nurse, "I can't understand it. Why did he do all that for me? He is a white man and I am an Indian. My own people threw me out; I can't understand it. I never heard of anything like this before." The Navajo nurse, a sweet Christian girl, said to her, "You know, it is the love of Christ that made him do that." "What do you mean by the love of Christ? Who is this Christ? Tell me more about Him." The nurse did not think that she could tell it in the right way

and so called the missionary. He sat down and
talked to her, and day by day unfolded the
wonderful story. After some weeks (for she
could take in only a little at a time) they thought
she understood enough to make her decision. They
had a special prayer-meeting for her, and then
gathered around that bed and prayed that God by
His Spirit would open her blind eyes. Again they
told the story, and then said, "Can't you trust this
Saviour, turn from the idols you have worshiped,
and trust Him as the Son of the living God?" She
looked at them with her big dark Indian eyes and
was silent a long time, and then the door yonder
opened and the doctor stepped in. Her face lit
up and she said, "If Jesus is anything like the
doctor, I can trust Him forever," and she came to
Christ. Do you see what had reached her? She
had seen divine love manifested in a man. That
is what you and I are called to exhibit to the
world.

"No man hath seen God at any time. If we
love one another, God dwelleth—abideth—in us,
and His love is perfected in us." That love which
was told out so fully in Jesus is now being manifested in those who have received life from the
risen Christ, and are thus called upon to make
known to the world for which He died, the same
wondrous love that led Him to go to the cross.
And so the apostle concludes this brief section by
saying, "Hereby know we that we dwell—abide—

in Him." That is, if we love in this divine way, we abide in Him. You cannot abide in Christ and have hatred in your heart; you cannot abide in Christ and have malice in your heart, have unlovely thoughts and unholy desires. All these break fellowship with the blessed Lord.

"Hereby know we that we abide in Him, and He in us, because He hath given us of His Spirit." Notice carefully these last words. Notice what John does not say, and then what he does say. The longer I live the more I am filled with admiration for this wonderful Book. It is absolutely perfect. I am asked sometimes what my theory of inspiration is. I tell them, "God spake all these words." All Scripture is divinely breathed. No other book will stand the rigid test that this will. Get one little word out of place and you have disjointed the whole thing. Many ask, "Do you believe in verbal inspiration?" Of course I do. *Verbo*—A word! What other inspiration could I believe in? I have to believe in verbal inspiration, that is, inspired words, if I believe in any inspiration at all. It is not merely the message that is from God; but the form, the words, of the message also.

God does not say here that He gives us His Spirit. It is perfectly true that He does, for we would not be Christians if He had not given us His Spirit: "If any man hath not the Spirit of Christ, he is none of His." But He is speaking to people here to whom He has already given His Spirit and telling them how they can manifest divine love. "Because He hath given us *of* His Spirit." What does that mean? He has Himself implanted within us something which He has given us *from* His Spirit. That is the new nature. His Spirit is that of love, and this is the very essence of the new nature, so that all you and I have to do is to let the Spirit of God control us, and as we do that, we will manifest the love of Christ.

Unsaved one, this seems like a high standard to you, and you say, "I do not see how I could ever live up to this, and what is more, I do not know that I have ever seen a Christian who did fully do so." Yes, I know I have failed to live up to it, but this is my objective, my desire, my aim, and it is better to have a splendid and high objective and fail to obtain it than to have a low one and go beyond it. But you might say, "If this is what is expected of a Christian, I am afraid I can never be one." An Indian once said to me, "Well, you know what I can see is this—Here we are in our sin and a great abyss is before us. On the other side is heaven. We must get from our sins over to heaven, and in order to do that there is a bridge across that chasm, but it is like a razor-edge, and I have to walk on that!" No, the wonderful thing is that Christ Himself has bridged the chasm and will carry you over from sin to salvation, from hell to heaven. And in order that we may manifest the love of Christ, He has given us His divine nature, and so it is not something that is impractical. We are called upon to receive Christ, and then He gives us the nature that delights to love. "Whosoever loveth —in this sense— is born of God."

Perfect Love that Casts Out Fear

"And we have seen and do testify that the Father sent the
Son to be the Saviour of the world. Whosoever shall confess that Jesus is the Son of God, God dwelleth in him, and
he in God. And we have known and believed the love that
God hath to us. God is love; and he that dwelleth in love
dwelleth in God, and God in him. Herein is our love
made perfect, that we may have boldness in the day of judgment: because as He is, so are we in this world" (1 John
4: 14-17).

We have already noticed that the manifestation
of divine love is the gift of the Lord Jesus Christ.
We had Christ presented to us in two different
ways in verses 9 and 10. Because we were dead
in trespasses and sins, the Father sent the Son
that we might live through Him. Because we are
guilty on account of our iniquity, God sent His
only begotten Son into the world to be the propitiation for our sins.

John sums it all up in verse 14 and says, "We
(the apostolic company) have seen (they who were
witnesses who knew Christ personally), and do
testify (bear witness) that the Father sent the
Son to be the Saviour of the world." Notice
again, "The Father sent the Son"—the relationship of Father and Son did not begin after Jesus

was born into the world; but from all eternity the
Father and the Son dwelt together in hallowed
fellowship.   Christ is the eternal Son.   He did
not become the Son after He was sent, but "the
Father sent the Son to be the Saviour of the
world."   This does not imply, of course, that all
men will be saved, but it does imply that God has
provided a Saviour for all men, so that the great
question between God and man to-day is not merely the question of our sins, or of our sinfulness by
nature, or our sins in practice, but the great question that is up between God and man is this,
"What are we doing with the Lord Jesus Christ?"

"God commendeth His own love toward us, in
that, while we were yet sinners, Christ died for
us" (Rom. 5:8).   If we have accepted Him, put
our trust in Him, then we know Him as Saviour.
If we reject Him, all His wondrous work goes for
nought as far as we are concerned, and only adds
to our condemnation.   But "whosoever shall confess that Jesus is the Son of God, God abideth
(dwelleth) in him, and he in God."   There is no
other meeting-place between God and man except
Christ Jesus.   To own Him as a great Teacher
does not save, to acknowledge Him as the greatest
among the sons of men does not bring deliverance;
but to own Him as Son of God, to put one's trust
in Him as Son of God, and thus confess Him
before men, this alone brings salvation.

You find the word *whosoever* used in John's

writings over and over again.   What an all-inclusive word it is!   We read in John 3: 16, that grand old verse that Luther called the miniature Bible, that "God so loved the world, that He gave His only begotten Son, that whosoever believeth in Him should not perish, but have everlasting life."   It is strange that any one should question the universality of the offer of mercy with a verse like that in the Bible.   "Whosoever believeth hath"—any one in any circumstances or conditions who puts his trust in the Lord Jesus Christ enters into the present possession of eternal life.   And so we read here, "Whosoever shall confess that Jesus is the Son of God, God dwelleth in him, and he in God."   Mark, it is "whosoever shall confess," not merely whosoever shall profess. There are a great many people who profess that they believe Jesus is the Son of God but they have never trusted Him as such.   You cannot confess Him as Son of God until He is your own Saviour.   You confess the One in whom you have trusted.   "If thou shalt confess with thy mouth the Lord Jesus, and shalt believe in thine heart that God hath raised Him from the dead, thou shalt be saved" (Rom. 10: 9).   But on the other hand, let us not forget that there is another very solemn "whosoever," and that is also found in the writings of John, "Whosoever was not found written in the book of life was cast into the lake of fire" (Rev. 20: 15).   Think of the solemnity of that declaration. It is the same word, *whosoever*. "Whosoever believeth...hath everlasting life," therefore the believer's name is inscribed in the book of life. Whosoever refuses to believe, whosoever will not put his trust in the Lord Jesus Christ, "whosoever" is "not found written in the book of life," must be banished eternally from the presence of God.

Consider it well. After all the gospel preaching you have listened to, after all the Christian people you have known through the years, are you among those who have never yet definitely received the Lord Jesus Christ into their own hearts? I beg of you do not defer the settlement of this question for even one hour. Just where you are, lift your heart to God, tell Him you are the sinner for whom Christ died, tell Him that you are coming to Him for the salvation which He has provided through His blessed Son, and that you are trusting Him, the Lord Jesus Christ, as your own Saviour. Then go forth to confess Him before men, for, "Whosoever shall confess that Jesus is the Son of God, God dwelleth in him— God abideth in him—and he in God."

"And we have known and believed the love that God hath to us." Have you? This is the declaration of faith, the declaration of one who has definitely laid hold of the gospel message for himself. "And we have known and believed the love that God hath to us. God is love." This is the second time that statement is made in this chapter. We have already considered it in verse 8: "He that loveth not, knoweth not God; for God is love." And now here again the Spirit reminds us that "God is love." This is His very nature, this is the very essence of His being; and "he that abideth in love abideth in God, and God in him." There you have fellowship in the light, according to the nature of God Himself. You cannot have fellowship with Him while harboring malice, unkindness, or hatred in your heart. It is impossible. All those things spring from that old corrupt nature inherited from Adam. But if converted we have received a new nature. We may sometimes forget Him for a time, and malice and envy and unkindness and hatred and all these evil things spring up anew; but as long as we are permitting any of these to bear sway in our lives, we are not abiding in love, and therefore not abiding in God, not living in fellowship with Him. Fellowship can only be enjoyed as we walk in light and in love.

Now that there may be no misunderstanding as to what this love is, he says in verse 17 (following the marginal reading), "Herein hath love with us been perfected, that we may have boldness in the day of judgment: because as He is, so are we in this world." I confess to you that there were years in my Christian life when I had the most confused ideas as to what these words really

meant, and yet today I know of no passage of
Scripture that gives me greater joy or seems
clearer, than this verse which puzzled me for so
long.   Shortly after I was converted, I pored over
it and said, "I can't understand it."   Of course
I was misled by the authorized reading, and did
not notice how beautifully it is corrected in the
margin.   I pored over the words, "Herein is our
love made perfect, that we may have boldness in
the day of judgment: because as He is, so are we
in this world," and I said to myself, "If boldness
in the day of judgment depends upon my love
being perfect, how can I ever be sure that everything will be right with me?"   I was looking at
myself and within my own heart for perfect love,
and as I searched that poor heart, I was always
finding something there that was contrary to perfect love, and I would say to myself, "Am I ever
going to be perfect in love?   I cannot have boldness in the day of judgment until my love is perfect." I would go to God and pray most earnestly,
would seek to make the fullest kind of surrender,
would ask Him to make me perfect in love, and
then get up and look within and say, "Let me see;
is it all right now?   Do I love everybody perfectly?"   And I would try to think I did.   Then
I would get out in the world again and find I did
not like this person and that one, and sometimes
little twinges of jealousy would spring up, and,
you know, you are never jealous of any one you

love, and never envious of any one you love, and so I would say, "I am just as bad as ever I was; how am I ever going to stand in the day of judgment?"

I found many other people in the same fix, and I would try to help them get this perfect love when I was not sure of it myself. But I thought you had to have it, and even though I had not the experience myself, I wanted to help others. One dear fellow came to the mourner's bench one night sobbing most bitterly. He had been converted for about two weeks, and I had known him first as a young bridegroom. I said, "What is the trouble?" He said, "I am trying to make a full surrender, but I can't seem to do it." I said, "What is the real difficulty?" "Well," he said, "I simply can't come to the place where I love every other woman as much as I do my wife, and as long as I love her more than anybody else, I realize it is selfish." "Now," I said, "you had better look out, young man. Start loving every other woman as much as you do your wife and you will surely get into trouble. God gave you that wife that you might love her above everybody else." "But," he said, "how can I have perfect love if I love her more than any one else?" What downright stupidity that was! And yet I did not know how to meet it!

It was like a second and even more glorious conversion than when I was first saved, when God showed me that perfect love is in another Man altogether. I had been looking for it in this man for six and one-half years after my conversion, and God one day turned me away from myself and said to me, "Look up there!" And by faith I saw another Man, the Man Christ Jesus, seated in highest glory at the Father's right hand, and God said to me, as it were, "There it is; perfect love is displayed in Christ." "Herein"—wherein? Why, "In this was manifested the love of God toward us, because that God sent His only begotten Son into the world, that we might live through Him." Wherein? "Herein is love, not that we loved God, but that He loved us, and sent His Son to be the propitiation for our sins." Wherein? In this, "We have seen and do testify that the Father sent the Son to be the Saviour of the world." "Oh," I said, "I see it at last. Perfect love led Christ to come from Godhead's fullest glory down to Calvary's depth of woe; perfect love led Jesus to look upon a lost, ruined, guilty world, take all our sins upon Him, and die in our place upon a felon's cross."

We sometimes sing a hymn, one line of which is, "I lay my sins on Jesus." I do nothing of the kind, and I will tell you why. It is too late to lay my sins on Jesus, and it is too late for you to do so, because 1900 years ago when Jesus hung a bleeding victim on Calvary's cross, the Lord "laid on Him the iniquity of us all." Bliss has written:

"What, lay my sins on Jesus,
  God's well-beloved Son?
No, 'tis a fact most precious
  That God e'en that hath done."

When did God do that? When Jesus died on Calvary. He made full atonement, and there perfect love was displayed in all its fulness.

But where is the One who took my sin and died on the cross? He is seated at the right hand of the majesty in the heavens. What about my sins? When He hung on the cross my sins were on Him; are they on Him now as He sits there? Impossible. He could not have entered heaven with *one* on Him. What then? Perfect love has settled the sin-question, has put my sins away forever, and now we may have boldness in the day of judgment." I am not afraid of the day of judgment now. Why not? Because my case is not coming up.

Suppose that passing a court-house you see a great throng gathered, and you ask what it all means. They reply, "There are some very important cases today of men charged with murder and other fearful crimes." You say, "I think I will go in," and somebody asks, "Why, aren't you afraid to go in there? Suppose they should lay hold of you." "Why should I be afraid?" you inquire; "my case is not going to be brought up. There is nothing against me. I am simply a spectator, an onlooker, a listener." Let

me say to the glory of the One who put away
my sins that when the Great White Throne is
set up and the wicked stand before that throne
to be judged for the deeds done in the body, I
shall be there with my blessed Lord, but I shall
not be there to be judged; I shall be there as a
spectator, as an onlooker, in association with the
Judge Himself.

Years ago we had a very odd judge out in
San Francisco, and tourists going through the city
would usually be taken to see Judge Campbell's
court.   One day a group of us were going through
the court-house, and in the party were four dis-
tinguished-looking ladies.   When the judge saw
them, he sent a bailiff after them, asking them
to come to the judge's seat.   They went up and
sat with him on the bench.   He would hear the
evidence, and then turn to the first lady and say,
"I will let you pronounce sentence."   "Well," she
would say, "I don't know what to do."   "This
offence would get from ten to thirty days," the
judge would say.   "Oh," she would reply, "don't
give him more than ten days."   "The lady says
you are to have ten days," the judge would answer.   Case after case of that kind came up while
the ladies were sitting there, but they "had boldness in the day of judgment."   Why?   Because
they were not being judged; they were associated
with the judge.   And, dear friends, when the
Great White Throne is set up, I am going to be

there in association with the Judge. "The world shall be judged by you," and I will tell you something more, I am going to see the devil who has caused me so much trouble throughout the years bound in chains and brought to my feet to know what I want done with him, for the Book says, "Ye shall judge angels." The lost angels will receive their sentence of judgment from the people of God. No wonder the Apostle Paul said, "The God of peace shall bruise Satan under your feet shortly" (Rom. 16:20). Yes, we have boldness in the day of judgment because perfect love has settled the sin-question. Jesus said in John 5:24, "Verily, verily, I say unto you, He that heareth My word, and believeth on Him that sent Me, hath everlasting life, and shall not come into condemnation; but is passed from death unto life." I like the Roman Catholic translation of that verse. The rendering of the Douai Version is, "Amen, amen, I say unto you, He who hears My word and believes Him who sent Me, has eternal life, and comes not into judgment, but is passed out of death into life." Is that not a wonderful message? It is enough to settle the question forever for any one who will believe. One who knows Christ has eternal life here and now, does not hope to have it eventually, but has it now, and shall never come into judgment, but is already passed out of death into life.

Then look at the rest of verse 17, "Herein hath

love with us been perfected that we may have
boldness in the day of judgment, because as He is,
so are we in this world." Some of the greatest
truths in the Word of God are packed into the
shortest and the simplest sentences. Sometimes
when preachers want to impress their audiences,
they use great swelling words that make things
sound profound. Some folk dote on that sort of
thing. This reminds me of the two Scotch women
who listened to the new preacher, and on the way
out, the one said to the other, "How did you like
the new preacher?" "Well, I thought he was
very good," was the reply. The other said, "He
was good, but could you understand him?" "I
would not presume to try to understand him," she
answered. Her idea was that a preacher ought to
use such grand language that it would be far above
them. A colored preacher was giving things out
in such a way that nobody could get the meaning,
and a brother spoke up and said, "Brother, put
the cookies on the lower shelf so the children can
reach them." Spurgeon used to say, "The Lord
said, 'Feed My sheep,' but some ministers have the
idea that He said, ' Feed My giraffes,' so they put
things so high that few can attain to them."

Here is one of the most profound truths of Holy
Scripture, and it is all embodied in nine monosyllables, and only three out of the nine have more
than two letters. "As He is, so are we in this
world." Nine monosyllables, and yet how pro-

found. I used to study it, but could not make it out. I would say, "I am not as holy as He is, I know that I am not as straightforward as He is, I am not as kind as He is, I am not as considerate of others as He is, I am not as tender and gracious as He is. What does it mean? 'As He is, so are we in this world.'" And I thought that it must be our ideal: "As He is, so ought we to be in this world." We are to aim at a star, and if we cannot hit it, it is better than it would be to aim at something lower. But no; that does not fit here. Well, then I thought it must be, "As He is, so shall we be when we get out of this world and get safe home to heaven." But that would not do. But what does it mean? It means exactly what it says, as Scripture always does. "As He is" —as who is? As Christ is. "So are we in this world." As Christ is in regard to what? Of what has he just spoken? As He is in relation to *judgment*. What is Christ's relation to judgment? Is He ever coming into judgment? Oh, no. Has He ever been there? Yes. When? When He died on Calvary for my sin. That was the judgment-day, and Christ settled everything for me that day, and now God has raised Him from the dead and taken Him to His own right hand, and there He sits exalted. As He is in relation to judgment so are we in this world. We do not have to wait until we get home to heaven and are absolutely perfect, as we shall be some

day, but right here and now we have the testimony
of the Word of God that we are just as secure
from judgment as He is because we are accepted
in Him.

> "So near, so very near to God,
>   I could not nearer be;
> For in the person of His Son
>   I am as near as He.
>
> "So dear, so very dear to God,
>   Dearer I could not be;
> The love wherewith He loved His Son,
>   Such is His love to me."

What an incentive to live for Him! What an
incentive to yield our lives as a living sacrifice
since He in grace has settled the whole question
of our justification, our acceptance with God, our
immunity from judgment!

Made Perfect in Love

"There is no fear in love; but perfect love casteth out fear: because fear hath torment. He that feareth is not made perfect in love. We love Him, because He first loved us, If a man say, I love God, and hateth his brother, he is a liar: for he that loveth not his brother whom he hath seen, how can he love God whom he hath not seen? And this commandment have we from Him, that he who loveth God love his brother also" (1 John 4:18-21).

We have noticed that perfect love is not something which is found in us. No Christian, no matter how devoted, how mature, has ever in himself manifested perfect love. There is some selfishness, some jealousy, some envy, some self-seeking in the heart of every child of God. Sometimes people imagine that they have gotten beyond all this, but circumstances soon bring out the fact that they have not. When we look for perfect love, we find it in our blessed Lord Jesus Christ, and we see that it was manifested when He in infinite grace gave Himself on the cross for guilty sinners such as we. It is the contemplation of this that banishes all our fear.

"There is no fear in love." You see, if it were a question of our own love, that could not be said, for every honest Christian would be continually in fear if he thought that his final acceptance depended upon his own inward perfection in love. He would say to himself, "Well, I have trusted the Lord Jesus Christ, and I hope everything is coming out all right at last, but my love is sometimes so cold, it is sometimes so low, that really I fear when the Lord makes inquisition He will find so much in me contrary to His mind that I will not be accepted at all." But, thank God, we are turned away from ourselves and from our experiences and directed to the full manifestation of perfect love in the cross. God says, as it were, "There you see love triumphant." Love manifested in all its fulness, reached down to the deepest depths and lifted up poor sinners utterly lost and ruined and undeserving, and so, depend upon it, He will never give you up. "Having loved His own which were in the world, He loved them unto the end" (John 13: 1).

"There is no fear in love." Watch a little child who really believes that you love it with all your heart, and how trustful that little one is. If you believe that "God so loved the world that He gave His only begotten Son, that whosoever believeth in Him should not perish, but have everlasting life," how can you ever fear that you may perish? How can you dread being shut out of heaven, for "perfect love casts out fear?"

"There is no fear in love; but perfect love casteth out fear; because fear hath torment." This word *torment* is used elsewhere in Scripture; it speaks of a grief, of a form of pain and anguish, of spiritual and mental distress which unsaved men and women have in this life, and which will go on eternally, if they leave this world in their sins.   I have often tried to make something clear which I am afraid I seldom succeed in making as plain as I should like to do, for every time I speak of it, I find somebody has misunderstood, and yet at the risk of being misunderstood, I am going to say a word about it.   The Holy Scriptures plainly teach that if men and women die in their sins, they are going to suffer consciously under the judgment of God for all eternity.   Now that is a very solemn thing, and it is a very sad thing. It is not something over which any of us gloat; it is not something in which any of us glory.   It moves our hearts to their deepest depths and might well stir us up to weep over lost men and women as the Lord did when He said, "Ye will not come to Me, that ye might have life" (John 5:40).   We read in the Word of God, "These shall go away into everlasting punishment" (Matt. 25:46), and, "Shall be tormented day and night for ever and ever" (Rev. 20:10).   There is no hint that their suffering will ever come to an end. But now having said that, I want to say that while the Word of God plainly teaches the eternal punishment of Christ-rejecters, it never even so much as hints at the eternal torture of lost men.   I say that because I think it is well that we should keep

God's character clear. There is nothing vindictive about God. He has no desire to inflict any unnecessary pain or anguish on men; He has nothing to "take out on" men, and so, Scripture never speaks, as preachers sometimes do, of eternal torture. That word is never used. God will never torture men, He will never permit the devil to torture them, He will never permit demons to torture them, and they will not be allowed to torture one another.

Hell is not a kind of pandemonium where wicked men and lost angels torture one another and sin against God for all eternity. It is God's well-ordered prison-house where men who never behaved before will have to behave at last, where "every knee shall bow...and every tongue confess that Jesus Christ is Lord, to the glory of God the Father" (Phil. 2:10, 11). Satan will not torture men, and he will not reign as king in hell. He will be the most abject being in the pit of woe. Hell was created for the devil and his angels, and it is his prison-house, where he will be in the lowest depths of the lake of fire, suffering for the sins he has committed throughout the ages. And so, every man will be judged according to his own sin and will suffer according to his own transgression. No statement is ever made in the Bible of the torture of lost souls. While Scripture never teaches that, it does teach the eternal torment of men who die impenitent.

I know that our English words, *torment* and *torture*, come from the same Latin root, which means *to writhe and twist in anguish*, but *torture* suggests the infliction of physical suffering, and *torment* is used for the suffering of the mind. "Fear hath torment." You know the awful anguish of mind that fear can throw you into. When you dread some terrible calamity, you know the torment into which you are cast. Here is a man who has shut his eyes to the perfect love of God, refused to believe the gospel testimony, and he sees rising before him the Great White Throne, and knows he must answer for his sins. He is rightfully filled with fear, and "Fear hath torment." If that man refuses to bow in repentance before God, and to accept the Lord Jesus Christ as his Saviour, and goes out of this life spurning the grace of God and trampling upon the precious shed blood of the Redeemer, then he goes out to be tormented forever. I think the most awful torment that can come to a lost soul in the pit of woe will be to think of days gone by, to remember mercies rejected, to meditate upon grace despised, and cry in the anguish of his soul, "Jesus died for me, and I knew all about it; He shed His precious blood for sinners, and I heard about it over and over again; He died for me, and I rejected Him; rejected His mercy, and here I am shut away from the light and joy of God for all eternity, and it is my own fault. I might have been saved, I might have been washed from my sins, but I refused to trust the Saviour that God provided, and now His wrath rests on me forever." I cannot imagine anything worse than that; and that, as I understand it, will be the very essence of the torment that lost men and women must endure for eternity.

We remember the word of Abraham to that once-rich man, "Son, remember!" All is wrapt up in that word, *remember* — remember for all eternity! Psychologists tell us that we never forget anything that we have ever known; it is all stored away in our minds. We may think we have forgotten, but you know how things will come to the surface when you least expect them. They come up before us when we are not even thinking of them, and so it will be with men in a lost eternity. Every sin, every iniquity, every transgression, every disobedience, will come up some day, and will remain throughout all the ages to come. Men will remember the follies of this life and how foolishly they treated God's offer of mercy. "Son, remember!"

I cannot leave that word without reminding you that for the righteous, too, that word, *remember*, has its place. We read, "Thou shalt remember all the way which the Lord thy God led thee" (Deut. 8:2). Memory for the child of God—what a blessed thing! Memory for the lost soul—what a fearful thing! God grant if you are still unsaved that in the light of the perfect love manifested in the cross, all your fears may be dissipated, that your torment may disappear, and your heart made to sing, "He loved me and gave Himself for me." This is the love that casts out fear.

Now John goes on to say, "He that feareth is not made perfect in love." Here is a little group of High School scholars in a Latin Class, and they know that next Monday there is to be a Latin examination. All day Saturday some of them have been cramming and cramming and endeavoring to get ready for the test, and they cannot even get their minds quieted on Sunday. What does that tell? It tells that they are not made perfect in Latin, and that they know that they are not. They would not be cramming or worrying if they knew their lesson. Here is another student in the class, a bright young girl who is neither cramming nor worried. One of the others meets her and says, "Don't you realize you have a Latin examination on Monday?"

"Yes."

"Well, don't you feel worried?"

"Not at all."

"Well, why is it that you are not anxious?"

"Because as the days and weeks have gone on I have been getting my lessons perfectly every day. I am thankful to have a good memory, and it is all stored away. and so I am not afraid now."

The one who is "perfect in Latin" is not afraid; the one who is not perfect in Latin is afraid.   If we are made perfect in love, we have learned our lesson and our fear is gone.   It is not my love that keeps; it is His love.

Now we come to the practical side in verse 19, and here I shall have to lift a word out of the text, for if you will consult the Greek you will find that one word does not appear.   It is omitted in all the older manuscripts. Correctly we read, "We love, because He first loved us."   Maybe some of you feel that you have lost something, you like to think, "We love *Him,* because He first loved us." But take it just as the Spirit of God originally wrote it, "We love, because He first loved us." Think it over, and you will see how much more precious that is after all.   Many a one will talk about loving Him who has not very much love for His!   How easy it is to talk about loving Christ and loving God, and yet be cold and unkind and discourteous toward those for whom Jesus died. The test of whether we really love Him is found in the way we behave toward His, and what a test that is!   You say you love Him, but you do not love Him a bit more than you love the child of God of whom you think the least.   Just try to think who that is, that cantankerous, cross-grained person who always seems to upset you, and yet you know that that one belongs to the

Lord Jesus Christ, that he is a member of Christ's Body. You do not love Christ any more than you love His members, and so, "We love, because He first loved us."

When our hearts are occupied with His wondrous love, we remember that He loved us when we were unlovely, and some of us are not very lovely now; we remember that He loved us when we were unlovable, and some of us are not very lovable yet. If He could do that when we were rebellious, and if that same love is now shed abroad in our hearts, we ought to be able to love those who are sinful and unkind and selfish. It is love triumphing in the midst of evil. "We love, because He first loved us."

Here is the last of the tests that John brings before us, "If a man say, I love God, and hateth his brother, he is a liar: for he that loveth not his brother whom he hath seen, how can he love God whom he hath not seen?" John uses very strong language sometimes. A great many people have a wrong idea of the apostle John. Many of the ecclesiastical pictures present him as a fair and effeminate-looking individual, and some think of him as one of these white-livered, milk-and-water sort of people, rather than a real vigorous man. That is a wrong idea. He was probably a young man about eighteen years old when he and his brother James came to Christ, for you know John was the youngest of the disciples. He died about A.D. 96, and at that time he was an aged man and could look back to the days of his youth when he walked with Jesus. Long after Paul and Peter and all the rest were with Christ, John was still ministering the Word at Ephesus, and afterward he was sent to Patmos because of his faithfulness in witnessing for Christ. He was true to the name given by Jesus long before. As the Lord looked at those two brothers, James and John, in their earnest youth, He said, "I am going to give you another name, I am going to call you Boanerges, the sons of thunder." There is nothing effeminate about that, and that is Jesus' own name for them.

On one occasion as they were going through Samaria James and John were so stirred up by the action of the Samaritans that they said, "Lord, wilt Thou that we command fire to come down from heaven, and consume them, even as Elias did?" (Luke 9: 54). You see the Samaritans at first were desirous to see them, but when they noticed that Jesus was anxious to get on to Jerusalem, they would have nothing to do with Him. They did not know that He was eager to go there in order to die for them, but thought He was not interested in them but rather in the people at Jerusalem, and so did not want Him. And because of this John and his brother would destroy them. But Jesus said to James and John, "Ye know not what manner of spirit ye are of" (Luke

9:55). There was nothing gentle about wanting to call fire down from heaven! John was not an effeminate kind of a young man; he was strong, vigorous and red-blooded.

Notice the strong language John uses. Turn back to chapter 2, verse 4, "He that saith, I know Him, and keepeth not His commandments, is a liar, and the truth is not in him." In verse 22 of the same chapter we read, "Who is a liar but he that denieth that Jesus is the Christ?" And now in verse 20 of chapter 4, John uses no fancy words but says, "If a man say, I love God, and hateth his brother, he is a liar: for he that loveth not his brother whom he hath seen, how can he love God whom he hath not seen?" The way you treat your brother, then, is the test as to whether you really love God.

"And this commandment have we from Him, that he who loveth God love his brother also." If you do not keep His commandments, you are not walking in obedience to His Word. "A new commandment I give unto you, That ye love one one another; as I have loved you, that ye also love one another" (John 13:34). We need to remember the word, "Let us not love in word, neither in tongue; but in deed and in truth" (1 John 3:18). Think of this the next time you feel provoked with somebody. Say to yourself, "How often I have grieved the Holy Spirit, but He loves me still. How often I have provoked the Lord, but He

loves me still.   How often I have dishonored the
Father, but He loves me still.   Blessed God, by
Thy Holy Spirit let that same divine all-conquering love be shed abroad in my heart, that I may
never think of myself but of others for whom
Christ has died, and be ready to let myself out
in devoted, loving service for their blessing." This
is Christianity in practice

Overcoming the World

"Whosoever believeth that Jesus is the Christ is born of God: and every one that loveth Him that begat loveth him also that is begotten of Him. By this we know that we love the children of God when we love God, and keep His commandments. For this is the love of God, that we keep His commandments: and His commandments are not grievous. For whatsoever is born of God overcometh the world: and this is the victory that overcometh the world, even our faith. Who is he that overcometh the world, but he that believeth that Jesus is the Son of God?" (1 John 5:1-5).

"Whosoever believeth that Jesus is the Christ, is born of God: and every one that loveth Him that begat, loveth him also that is begotten of Him." The direct occasion for so writing is found in the closing verses of the former chapter, where we read, "If a man say, I love God, and hateth his brother, he is a liar."

One is likely to ask, "But who do you mean by my brother?" Some people have an idea that our brethren are those who happen to belong to the same particular company with whom we associate. If I belong to one certain church, my brethren are those who go to that church; that is, if I am a Methodist, my brethren are Methodists; if I am a Presbyterian, my brethren are Presbyterians; if I am a Baptist, my brethren are the immersed, and perhaps not all the immersed, for some of them may have undergone alien-immersion, and so as they are not the particular ones with whom I associate, they are not my brethren! Our poor minds are inclined to narrow down the brotherhood to some special fellowship, some group of assemblies with which we are linked. But in this fifth chapter the Lord Himself gives the limits of the brotherhood when He says, "Whosoever believeth that Jesus is the Christ, is born of God: and every one that loveth Him that begat, loveth him also that is begotten of Him." The brethren include all in every place who have exercised faith in the Lord Jesus Christ; because by this expression, "Whosoever believeth that Jesus is the Christ," we are not to understand a mere intellectual acceptance of the creedal fact that Christ is the Son of the living God, but rather a true, vital confidence—personal faith in the Lord Jesus as the Christ, the anointed One of God. If you have faith in Him, you are born of God. All who trust in Him enter into this relationship. It is not a question with whom you may associate, what church connection you may have; for, after all, there is only one great Assembly, the Body of Christ, which God Himself recognizes as His Church. We speak in a limited way with regard to church-membership, for we think of a local fellowship, yet when the Word of God speaks of this, it means that vast company of which Christ is the glorified Head in heaven. To that Church every believer belongs, every member of the family of God in this present age, and so as we ask, "Who is my brother?" we look out upon the whole Church of God and realize that our love must go out to them all.

"Whosoever believeth that Jesus is the Christ, is born of God: and every one that loveth Him that begat, loveth him also that is begotten of Him." There is no use talking about loving the Father if you do not love the Father's children; there is no use talking about our devotion to the Lord Jesus Christ if we are not devoted to those for whom He died. Love is a very real and practical thing. We speak of it in such a sentimental way sometimes and say, "I love all the people of God," but how do we prove it? What form does our love take? Scripture says, "Love suffereth long, and is kind; love vaunteth not itself, is not puffed up...beareth all things, hopeth all things, endureth all things" (1 Cor. 13: 4-6). Take some of these simple statements and test your own love to find where you stand. Are you envious of any of God's people? When honors come to others which do not come to you, do you rejoice in them? Scripture says, "Whether one member suffer, all the members suffer with it; or one member be honored, all the members rejoice with it" (1 Cor. 12: 36). When people are saying good things about somebody else and not saying them about you, does your heart rejoice in that? Are you thankful to see others honored and exalted, even though you may be left in the place of the one who is passed over? Real love of the brethren will lead to that very thing. It will always endeavor to put somebody else forward instead of oneself.

Love is active; love leads one to seek to serve, to delight to minister. Are you trying to serve the people of God or are you one of those who love to be served? Some Christians are always wanting others to do for them, and then there are Christians who are always trying to do for others. You know which are the happier of the two. The folk that are constantly looking for attention are never happy. They are ever feeling hurt and slighted. But with those who are manifesting the love of Christ, how different! Someone once said to me, "I go to such and such a place, but they are a cold lot there. I never see any love manifested," and I said, "Do you ever show any?" He looked at me and said, "Well, perhaps not as much as I should." Standing right near was another who attended the same place, and I said, "How do you find them down there?—a pretty cold lot?" "Why," she said, "I think they are one of the most loving and affectionate groups of Christians I have ever seen." She was showing love to them, and because of that she was getting good returns. You find what you are looking for.

Some time ago I read of a man who spent a few

months in India. When he came back, he was discussing India at the home of some of his friends, and the talk drifted to missions, and this man, out of his wide experience, about five months in India, said, "I have no use for missions and missionaries. I spent months there, and didn't see that they were doing anything; in fact, in all that time I never met a missionary. I think the church is wasting its money on missions." A quiet old gentleman sat near. He had not said anything, but now spoke up and said, "Pardon me; how long did you say you were in India?"

"Five months."

"What took you there?"

"I went out to hunt tigers."

"And did you see any tigers?"

"Scores of them."

"It is rather peculiar," said the old gentleman, "but I have spent thirty years in India, and in those years I never saw a tiger but I have seen hundreds of missionaries. You went to India to hunt tigers and you found them. I went to India to do missionary work and found many other missionaries."

Some have said to me, "I have come here for months and nobody ever shakes hands with me," and I say to them, "How many have you shaken hands with?" Love is a practical thing—"Every one that loveth Him that begat, loveth him also that is begotten of Him." Scripture also says,

"Love covereth all things." And again, "Love covereth a multitude of sins." It is translated *charity,* but it is really *love.* People seem to think of it as though it meant almsgiving.

In a saloon in Sacramento, California, I was giving out gospel messages one night to the people who drank and caroused there. I gave a little booklet to a well-dressed gentleman, and by and by he said to me, "Pardon me, sir, what church do you represent?" I told him, and he said, "I was interested in getting this little book; I am a church-member myself."

"You are in rather a bad place tonight," I said. "I am here serving the Lord; what are you here for?"

"Oh, I guess I slipped up a little tonight, but you know, a poor woman stopped me on the street just now, and asked me for a dime to get some coffee and doughnuts."

"And what did you do for her?"

"I gave her half-a-dollar. Don't you think that should cover up any little peccadilloes here this evening?"

He thought that the charity he had shown would cover up his drinking. But these words mean that if you know that your brother or your sister has failed, if you know of some sin, even some grievous sin that has come into their lives, you will never mention it to anybody but God, if you really love them, unless you go direct to them and try to help recover them first of all—"Love covereth all things." You will never be a talebearer, you will never be a gossip, never go about talking against your brother. When you know of anything wrong, you will go to God about it. The difference is this, when you talk to other people about your brother, you only spread things around and hurt the whole company, but when you go to God, the Holy Spirit of God can, in answer to your prayer, begin to work upon the heart and conscience of the wrong-doer, and he will be brought to repentance or be broken down under the discipline of the Lord. Of course there is something even higher than that. Love in all its fulness will lead you to go to that brother and tenderly, graciously, kindly, seek to help him in his trouble, point out the wrong, offer to pray with him, and leave it there with God if he bows in penitence before Him.

There is a beautiful little picture in the Old Testament in connection with the candlestick. The candle was really a little olive-oil lamp with a wick. The wick would burn just so long, and then turn over charred and blackened, needing to be snuffed. The Lord told Moses to make a golden candlestick with seven lamps, and its snuffers and the snuff-dishes of pure gold. The more I read my Bible the more I am impressed with the importance of every word. What is there in snuffers and snuff-dishes? Well, you see if a lamp is going to shine brightly,

it needs to be snuffed sometimes, and if I want
to burn brightly for Christ, there will be
many a time when I have to judge myself in the
presence of God, or I will be just like the burned
wick which obscured the light. The priest of old
was to go in and trim the lamp and use a golden
snuffer, and gold in Scripture speaks of that which
is divine, so the believer who reproves his brother
is to go to him in fellowship with God. I may be
able to help my brother if I go in tenderness and
grace. What did the priest do with that snuff
when he took it away? Did he scatter it all
around, get it on his white robe, and on his hands,
and go around defiling the garments of other
priests? Oh, no; he was to take that dirty black
snuff and put it in a golden snuff-dish, and cover
it up so that it would not defile anybody else. That
is what love does. You do not spread abroad your
brother's failures, you just show real love, and
cover them up in the presence of God. That is
love in a practical sense.

But now the second verse suggests something
more. "By this we know that we love the children of God, when we love God, and keep His
commandments." What a queer Book the Bible
is! First, John says, that we know we love God
because we love the brethren; and now he says,
"By this we know that we love the children of
God, when we love God." It seems illogical, like
reasoning in a circle, does it not? But God is

above all your rules of logic. He is not concerned
about them. That is why you can find so many
illogical things in the Bible, according to man's
mind. The Bible contains the truth regarding
predestination, but it also teaches the great truth
of man's responsibility, and shows us, as D. L.
Moody used to say, that the elect are the "whosoever wills," and the non-elect are the "whosoever
won'ts." This too seems to be reasoning in a
circle, but some day we shall see that all is perfect and harmonious.

And so with what we have before us here. If
we love God, we love the children of God also. If
we love the children of God we keep His commandments. Love is faithful. It does not make
light of sin. It does not seek to excuse evil. It
leads us to put the truth of God first and to bring
all else into subjection to it. I do not love my
brother when I condone his wrong-doing, or agree
(for the sake of peace) to what is in direct opposition to the command of God. Take the question of divorce and remarriage. There may be
circumstances where people have to be separated,
but if so, they are to remain unmarried (unless
divorced for clear scriptural reasons), and yet
what a lot of preachers there are who marry people who have been divorced contrary to the Word
of God. Some ministers may say, "I love these
people so much I don't want to hurt their feelings," but they are helping them to do something

that is contrary to the Word of God. That is not love. "By this we know that we love the children of God when we love God and keep His commandments." When we put the will of God first and seek to manifest love to His people, seek to do it in accordance with His Word, and lead our brethren in the path of obedience to the Word, that is real Christian love.

"For this is the love of God, that we keep His commandments: and His commandments are not grievous." But somebody says, "It is all very well to say that, but I find it dreadfully hard to do some things that God wants me to do." If I felt that way, I should begin to wonder whether I were really born again. If unsaved I have only one nature, and that nature hates the things of God. If you are born again, you have a new nature and you ought to glory in the will of God; and you will do so if you are walking in the power of an ungrieved Spirit. If you are a Christian and do not find delight in the will of God, it is because you are grieving the Holy Spirit, because there is something in your life that is dishonoring the Lord, and so you have lost your joy. Judge everything in your life that is contrary to the word of God, and you will be surprised to find how sweet His will is. You come to the crossroads and know that God's will is this way and your will is the other way. You know His way will mean happiness and that your way will bring misery. You may try your own way only to find that you are heaping wretchedness upon wretchedness, instead of finding true joy and peace. "His commandments are not grievous."

"For whatsoever is born of God (that new nature, that new life which is communicated to you) overcometh the world." It is a very blessed fact that every true believer will be an overcomer at the last, but I am afraid some of us, like Jacob, will never be overcomers until we are almost at the end of life. Jacob had been a child of God for many years, but it was not until he was down to the very end that he manifested the graces that God was seeking to work in him throughout all those years. Then we read, "By faith Jacob, when he was a-dying, blessed the sons of Joseph; and worshipped, leaning upon the top of his staff" (Heb. 11: 21). By faith when he was dying he was brought to the place of an overcomer. What a pity to have lost that past time, and what a pity if you and I should be so set upon having our own way that we should lose out throughout the years, years that can never be recalled.

What does it mean to overcome the world? All that is in the world is taken up in the second chapter of this epistle, the lust of the flesh, which is carnal indulgence of any kind; the lust of the eyes, or the pleasures of the senses, the esthetic pleasures; and then the pride of life, ambition, struggling after fame and praise in the world.

These are the things that constitute "the world."
Some Christians have the idea that worldliness
consists in going to the theatre, playing cards,
dancing, taking part in certain worldly pleasures.
No doubt these minister to one form of worldliness, the lust of the flesh and perhaps the lust of
the eye; but you may never have crossed the
threshold of a theatre, you may never sit down
at the card-table, you may never have been on the
dance-floor in your life, and yet you may be just
as worldly as the people who do these things. The
lover of money is as worldly as the lover of pleasure, of fame, of ambition. The one who is trying to crush others and push himself to the front
is just as worldly as the man who spends half
the night at the theatre. Do not think that you
can "compound for sins you are inclined to by
damning those you have no mind to." Overcoming the world means being delivered from the lust
of the flesh, the lust of the eye, and the ostentation
of living. As you obey the desires of the new
nature you are set free from the world, because
this new life rises up to God as water to its source
and finds delight in the things of God.

"And this is the victory that overcometh the
world, even our faith." In Revelation we hear
the Lord saying seven times over in His command
to write to the seven churches, "To him that overcometh." He is not singling out a superior class
of Christians, but means that in every age the

real Christians will be the overcomers, for by faith they overcome the world at last in every instance.

And now lest we should make any mistake about that, the fifth verse says, "Who is he that overcometh the world, but he that believeth that Jesus is the Son of God?" Do you believe that? Again I repeat, It is not merely as accepting a statement of creed, but it is that you trust in the blessed Son of God who came from the Father's bosom, went to Calvary's cross, and there shed His precious blood to put away your sins. Have you trusted Him? Have you believed on Him? Peter says, "Being born again, not of corruptible seed, but of incorruptible, by the word of God, which liveth and abideth for ever...And this is the Word which by the gospel is preached unto you" (1 Pet. 1: 23-25). When you believe the message of the gospel, when you receive the Lord Jesus Christ, the Son of God, as your personal Saviour, then you are born of God, then you have this new nature, then that faith is yours which is manifested by love. You may be sure of this; whatever failures, struggles, temptations you may have to meet, you will come through at last triumphant, because it is He that will bring you through. It is not a question of your own power or steadfastness, but you are "kept by the power of God, through faith unto salvation ready to be revealed in the last time" (1 Pet. 1: 5).

The Three Witnesses

"This is He that came by water and blood, even Jesus Christ; not by water only, but by water and blood. And it is the Spirit that beareth witness, because the Spirit is truth. For there are three that bear record in heaven, the Father, the Word, and the Holy Ghost: and these three are one. And there are three that bear witness in earth, the Spirit, and the water, and the blood: and these three agree in one. If we receive the witness of men, the witness of God is greater: for this is the witness of God which He hath testified of His Son. He that believeth on the Son of God hath the witness in himself: he that believeth not God hath made him a liar; because he believeth not the record that God gave of His Son. And this is the record that God hath given to us eternal life, and this life is in His Son. He that hath the Son hath life; and he that hath not the Son of God hath not life. These things have I written unto you that believe on the name of the Son of God; that ye may know that ye have eternal life, and that ye may believe on the name of the Son of God" (1 John 5:6-13).

We have before us in this section the three witnesses. I do not think that I need to take very much time pointing out the fact that we do not actually have six witnesses in this chapter; that is, three in heaven and three on earth. The seventh verse reads, in our Authorized Version: "For there are three that bear record in heaven, the Father, the Word, and the Holy Ghost: and these three are one." This is not found in any critical translation of the New Testament. My statement may trouble some of you who have never looked into this question, and you may say, "What, is there some part of Scripture that cannot be depended upon?" Let me try to explain, very briefly.

You must remember that the Bible was translated into English from Hebrew and Greek sources, that is, the Hebrew and Greek were handwritten and came down through the centuries, copied first by one and then by another, and it is quite possible for one man writing a manuscript to insert or to leave something out. It is quite possible for something to be put in the margin of one manuscript which the next scribe may take for granted belongs to the text. The oldest Greek manuscripts from which the King James' Version was taken were probably written in the twelfth century of the Christian era. Since then literally thousands of manuscripts have come to light from as far back as the end of the second and the beginning of the third century of the Christian era, and in none of them are these words found. The way they got in was probably because some scribe made a little comment on the margin of his manuscript, and then some one copying it thought those words belonged to the text, and so inserted them. This is a question that can easily be looked up.

In verse 6 we read, "This is He (that is, the Lord Jesus Christ of whom he spoke in verse 5), that came by water and blood, even Jesus Christ; not by water only, but by water and blood. And it is the Spirit that beareth witness, because the Spirit is truth." And now verse 8 reads, "And there are three that bear witness in earth, the Spirit, and the water, and the blood: and these three agree in one." What does the apostle mean when he speaks of these three that bear witness? —witness, in the sense of testimony. Three that give testimony—give testimony to what? Why, to the efficacy of the work of our Lord Jesus Christ. Three witnesses, the Spirit, the water, and the blood.

The Spirit, of course, is the Holy Spirit of God who, after the death, the resurrection, and the ascension of our Lord Jesus Christ, came from heaven to dwell in the Church on earth, to be the power for testimony as the missionaries of the cross go through all the lands of the world proclaiming the finished work of our Lord Jesus Christ. You know there is a vast difference between merely explaining the doctrines and preaching the gospel in the Spirit's power. Any man might do the former, and everything he said might be true, but there might be no power in it; but preaching the gospel in the energy of the Holy Ghost is another thing altogether; and therefore we read, "It pleased God by the foolishness of preaching to save them that believe" (1 Cor. 1:21). Jesus said, "Ye shall receive power, after that the Holy Ghost is come upon you; and ye shall be witnesses unto Me, both in Jerusalem, and in all Judea, and in Samaria, and unto the uttermost parts of the earth" (Acts 1: 8). The Holy Spirit, then, is a witness to the efficacy of the cleansing power of the precious blood of Christ. He has come down from the heavenly sanctuary to assure us that Christ has gone in, and His sacrifice has been accepted for us.

The other witnesses are the water and the blood. You will remember that in John's Gospel we are told that when they broke the legs of the thieves who hung on the crosses at either side of the Lord Jesus Christ, they looked upon the body of Jesus and marveled because He was already dead, and so they did not break His legs, for it was written, "A bone of Him shall not be broken" (John 19: 36). But one of the soldiers pierced His side with a spear, and, John writes, "Forthwith came there out blood and water" (John 19: 34). Now that made a great impression on the mind of John as he saw those two elements mingled and flowing from the wounded side of the Saviour.

Years had passed, and John, an old man, sat down to write this epistle to the children of God, and in it he says, "This is He that came by water and blood, even Jesus Christ; not by water only, but by water and blood." Why does he draw our attention to the water and the blood which flowed from the side of the Son of God? In these two elements we have suggested two characters of cleansing.

As a poor sinner in all the guilt of my transgressions, my awakened conscience yearns to be justified before the throne of God, and I learn that the blood of Jesus Christ cleanses from all sin. But that cleansing is judicial, that is my cleansing before God. As God looks at me as a believer, He sees me cleansed from every stain by the precious blood of His Son, but that alone does not satisfy me. My exercised heart as a Christian wants to know practical deliverance from the power of sin. I am not content to know that my sins have been put under the blood, if I find that I am still living under the power of sin. I want sin to be taken away practically. I want to be set free, to be cleansed from the things that curse my life; and I find practical cleansing through the "washing of water by the Word." We read in Ephesians 5: 25, 26, "Christ loved the Church, and gave Himself for it; that He might sanctify and cleanse it with the washing of water by the Word." The Word of God applied to my heart and conscience sets me free from sin as a habit. I am delivered from its power. Our Christian poet understood this when he wrote:

> "Let the water and the blood,
> From Thy riven side which flowed,
> Be of sin the double cure,
> Save me from its guilt and power."

The blood cleanses from sin's guilt, and the water of the Word applied in the power of the Holy Spirit cleanses from the defilement of sin, So then these are the three witnesses. The blood witnesses that the sin-question is settled to God's satisfaction, the Word witnesses that there is power to deliver me from sin in a practical way, and the Spirit bears witness that all this is for every believer in the Lord Jesus Christ.

"If we receive the witness of men (and we do); the witness of God is greater: for this is the witness of God, which He hath testified of His Son." There is one Greek word in this chapter which is translated by three English words, *witness, record, testimony.* I shall use the one English word, *witness,* throughout. "There are three that bear witness in earth, the Spirit, and the water, and the blood: and these three agree in one." They agree that there is full and complete salvation and life eternal for every believer in Christ. "If we receive the witness of men, the witness of God is greater." Men come to us and tell of things we have never seen, and we believe them. They make us promises upon which we rest. The entire commercial system of the world depends largely on the witness of men. They make certain promises, and we believe that they will if possible fulfil them, and because we trust them we go ahead and do business with them. If we are willing thus to trust our fellow-men who all may fail, who may go back on their pledges, and whose witness may prove to be untrue, surely we may say, "The witness of God is greater." God has given us a witness, and His witness can be relied upon. It is impossible for God to lie. The witness is His Word.

"For this is the witness of God, which He hath witnessed of His Son." Do you ask what it is of which the apostle is speaking? It is not a happy feeling in our hearts. People talk about having the witness of the Spirit, and they mean that they feel happy. You may feel happy today, and then tomorrow you may eat something that does not agree with you and feel miserable. Does that mean that you have lost the witness? Not at all. The witness is that which God has witnessed concerning His Son. In other words, God in His Word, by the Spirit, has given a testimony concerning His blessed Son. What has He told us about Him? He has told us that the blessed Lord Jesus died on the cross for our sins, that He "was delivered for our offences, and was raised again for our justification" (Rom.4:25). This is God's witness, and now He calls upon us to believe it.

In verse 10 we read, "He that believeth on the Son of God hath the witness in himself: he that believeth not God hath made Him a liar; because he believeth not the witness that God gave of His Son." I often meet people who say, "I think I believe in the Lord Jesus Christ, but I have been waiting for the witness, and some way or another it does not seem to come. I do not have the witness that my sins are forgiven." "This is the witness, that God hath given to us eternal life, and this life is in His Son." "He that believeth on the Son of God hath the witness in himself." It is not a question of feeling happy, it is not a question of a great emotional break-down or something like that; it is not a question of "getting religion," as people say; but it is a question of believing God and receiving His Word into the heart. When you do that, you have the witness in yourself, the Spirit of God makes it real to you, the Spirit of God gives you to know that it is indeed the very Word of the living God, and you rest on it. When asked, "Are you saved?" you may answer, "Yes." If they inquire, "How do you know?" you say, "Because God has told me so." You do not know you are saved because you feel happy. Not that at all; but you feel happy because you know you are saved. People so often put the cart before the horse, they look for feeling and happiness as a testimony that they are saved, when they must first believe the Word. Then the joy will follow.

Alex. Marshall, the Scotch evangelist, now with Christ, went many years ago as a young lad to a circus where a servant of Christ was preaching. He sat away yonder in one of the balconies, and he was anxious to be saved. He kept saying, "If I could only get the happy feeling that some of these people have, I would know it was all right with me." You know sometimes the Spirit of God gives the preacher just the right message for somebody in the audience, and this preacher leaned over the pulpit, and pointing to where this lad sat, he said, "Young man, believing is the root, feeling is the fruit." That moment the lad saw the whole thing and passed out of death into life. "He that believeth on the Son of God hath the witness in himself." You take God at His word and say, "Let God be true and every man a liar," and you may rest upon His Word.

On the other hand a man may say: "Oh, well; I do believe on Christ, but I would not dare say that I am saved. I am waiting for feeling, I am waiting for the witness." This is what God says, "He that believeth not God hath made Him a liar; because he believeth not the record that God gave of His Son." You may think you are honoring God when you say, "Well, I would like to believe, but some way I don't feel sure. If I could only have a different feeling come over me, it would be all right." But so long as you talk like that you are making God a liar. God has told you something which He asks you to believe. What does it imply if you do not believe? Suppose I should come to you and tell you something and you should say, "Yes; well, I would like to believe you, I am even trying to believe you; but some way or another

I cannot believe you." What would that mean? It would imply that you really thought I was lying to you, and it is just the same when you treat God's Word like that.

"He that hath the Son hath life." Do you say, "I am trying to believe?" Trying to believe whom? "Well, I am trying to believe that I am saved." Oh, no; that is not it. God's Word says, "Believe on *the Lord Jesus Christ*, and thou shalt be saved" (Acts 16:31). You might believe that you are saved, and not be saved at all, never have eternal life, but you cannot believe in the Lord Jesus Christ, in the sense of trusting in Him, without being saved, without having everlasting life. When you say, "I am trying to believe," you are making God a liar, because you do not believe "the record that God gave of His Son." What is that record? It is the witness about which we are talking.

A friend of mine who died some years ago in India did not have the assurance of salvation. The thing that troubled him above everything else was that he had an idea that God had chosen an elect few that should be saved, and as he had no evidence that he was among them, he could not know that he was saved. He went to a meeting where the preacher declared that a man was saved the moment he believed in Jesus, and that he possessed eternal life and could never perish. "Now," he said, "I would like to be sure of that."

When he got home, he got down on his knees **and**
prayed, "O God, if it is possible for a man to be
sure he has eternal life, show it to me now from
Thy own Word; but if it is not possible, show me
that, and I will leave it with Thee." He turned
to this fifth chapter of First John and read the
verses that I have read to you, and when he came
to the verse, "He that believeth not God hath made
Him a liar; because he believeth not the record
that God gave of His Son," he said, "I don't want
to make Him a liar, but I don't know what that
record is." And so he looked at the next verse,
and read, "And this is the record." He put his
thumb down on the rest of the verse, and shut his
eyes and prayed, "O God, I have just been reading
that if a man does not believe the record that
Thou hast given of Thy Son, he makes Thee a liar;
I don't want to make Thee a liar, but I don't know
what the record is. I suppose I have it under my
thumb. I am going to lift my thumb, and when I
do, help me to believe whatever I find there, because I do not want to make Thee a liar." He
almost dreaded to lift his thumb, but finally did,
and read, "And this is the record, that God hath
given to us eternal life, and this life is in His
Son." "Oh," he said, "blessed be God! Then
right here and now I can know!" and his faith
was confirmed as he read, "He that hath the Son,
hath life; and he that hath not the Son of God
hath not life." He saw that it was just a question

of receiving Him. He came into peace, and for years preached this same truth to others.

"He came unto His own, and His own received Him not. But as many as received Him, to them gave He power to become the sons of God, even to them that believe on His name" (John 1: 11, 12). Have you received Christ? Then, "He that hath the Son hath life." Are you rejecting Him? "He that hath not the Son of God hath not life." If the Son of God has not been received by faith as Saviour, you are still dead in trespasses and sins, but if you have received Him as your Saviour, God says you have everlasting life. Take Him at His word.

"These things have I written unto you that believe on the name of the Son of God; that ye may know that ye have eternal life, even you who believe on the name of the Son of God." Do you believe on the name of the Son of God? It is not an intellectual thing of which he speaks. Do you have faith in the Son of God? Do you trust in Him? Listen, then; I have a message for you, and I wish it would come home to every heart with power as if you had never heard it before. Suppose a letter came, and on its envelope you read, "To you who believe on the name of the Son of God." I say, "A letter has been handed to me, and if the person to whom it is addressed is here, please come and claim it. It is addressed to 'You who believe.'" What would you say? Do you believe on the name of the Son of God? Is the letter for you? Very well, then; let us open it and see what it says. "That ye may *know* that ye *have* eternal life, even you who believe on the name of the Son of God." It is a message from the high court of heaven to every believer in the Lord Jesus Christ.

Have you been doubting all through the years, have you been as the old colored song puts it, "Sometimes up and sometimes down," yet hoping all the while that you are heaven-bound, but not very sure of it? Get it settled today, put away your doubts and fears, and look by faith at the risen Christ. Take it from the blessed God Himself that "He that believeth on the Son hath everlasting life."

Faith's Confidence

———

"And this is the confidence that we have in Him, that, if we ask any thing according to His will, He heareth us: and if we know that He hear us, whatsoever we ask, we know that we have the petitions that we desired of Him. If any man see his brother sin a sin which is not unto death, he shall ask, and he shall give him life for them that sin not unto death. There is a sin unto death: I do not say that he shall pray for it. All unrighteousness is sin: and there is a sin not unto death. We know that whosoever is born of God sinneth not; but he that is begotten of God keepeth himself, and that wicked one toucheth him not. And we know that we are of God, and the whole world lieth in wickedness. And we know that the Son of God is come, and hath given us an understanding, that we may know Him that is true, and we are in Him that is true, even in His Son Jesus Christ. This is the true God, and eternal life. Little children, keep yourselves from idols. Amen" (1 John 5:14-21).

We have traced our way along from chapter one, and have noticed how marvelously God has come out in grace in the Person of His own blessed Son, our Lord Jesus Christ, how fully the sin-question has been settled, how completely the believer is purged from every stain and fitted for the immediate presence of God. We have seen how those who put their trust in Christ are brought out from under Satanic domination, are

regenerated by the Spirit and the Word, and
brought into the family of God, and how in this
family there is growth as one becomes better acquainted with the Lord and better acquainted with
the Word, so that the child of God moves on from
day to day, week to week, month to month, and
year to year, from spiritual childhood to spiritual
manhood, and eventually fatherhood. We have
noticed too how the two natures are still in the
believer, but how the Spirit of God gives us power
to act in the new nature and be preserved from
sin, how the love of God has been fully manifested
in the cross of Christ, perfect love triumphing
over all evil and over all sin and iniquity, casting
out all our fear, and giving us boldness in view
of judgment.

We have listened to the warnings of the Holy
Spirit to beware of by-paths and false teachings,
that would destroy our fellowship with God and
hide the glory of the Saviour's face. We have
seen how assurance comes through the Word,
through believing the message that God has sent;
but, on the other hand, how upon believing we
have an inward assurance based upon what the
Holy Spirit has wrought within, so that now we
love the brethren and delight in obedience to the
commands of God. We who were once hateful
and loved our own way and found the teachings
of God's Word distasteful, have now the witness
within that we have been accepted in Christ be-

cause our hope, our confidence, is based upon His finished work.

And now in these closing verses we have first a word as to the confidence of faith, of prayers heard and answered, and then a message as to those who sin unto death, and finally, in verses 18 to 21, the apostle epitomizes the teaching of the entire epistle.

In verses 14 and 15 we read, "This is the confidence that we have in Him, that, if we ask anything according to His will, He heareth us: and if we know that He hear us, whatsoever we ask, we know that we have the petitions that we desired of Him." The ordinary word for confidence in the New Testament is the same Greek word as is generally translated *faith*, but the word used here is a different one. The apostle is not simply saying, "This is the *faith* that we have in Him," or, "This is the *trust* that we have in Him," but he uses a word that literally means *boldness*: "This is the *boldness* that we have in Him, that, if we ask anything according to His will, He heareth us."

What a bold thing it is for a man or a woman once a poor sinner condemned to die under the judgment of God, but now redeemed by the precious blood of Christ, to dare to come into the presence of the infinite God, bringing the petitions that His Holy Spirit presses upon his heart and knowing that if he brings these to Him, inasmuch as they are in accordance with His will, "He heareth us." This is a boldness that the world cannot understand. Men and women who do not know Christ ask, "Do you think that your puny prayers, your petitions, are going to change the mind of Divine Omnipotence, and that God, the Infinite, is going to wait upon your pleadings, a poor finite creature so small that you are but as the dust of the balance in His sight?" Abraham felt something like that, and yet boldly came unto God and said, "O God, suffer Thy servant to speak to Thee, though he be but dust and ashes before Thee." And because he came in faith and in accordance with the will of God, his prayer was heard. So today we who know Him as our Saviour have this boldness, so we come to Him knowing that, "If we ask anything according to His will, He heareth us."

You may say, "Well, how do you know whether your petition is in accordance with His will?" That is a very important question. A prayer to be in accordance with the will of God must first of all be in accordance with the Word of God. I might pray, and pray earnestly, but my pleadings would never be heard if contrary to the Word of God. But then on the other hand I might even pray in accordance with the Word of God, but if I am not living in the will of God my prayer still goes unanswered, for, "If I regard iniquity in my heart, the Lord will not hear me" (Ps. 66:18). We read, "If ye abide in Me, and My words abide in you, ye shall ask what ye will, and it shall be done unto you" (John 15:7). Under such circumstances, God's will becomes our will, and so as we ask according to His will, we know He heareth us. "And if we know that He hear us, whatsoever we ask (that is, of course, whatsoever we ask in accordance with His will), we know that we have the petitions that we desired of Him."

We may not get the answer to our petitions immediately, we may not see our prayers answered on the moment, but if in accordance with the will of God, if in fellowship with God as we bring the petition, we may be definitely assured that He has heard and has answered, and that sometime, somewhere, we shall see the answer. Of course, we have to remember our human limitations, for we do not know always what is wise or best, and therefore we must be prepared to find that the answer sometimes comes in a way we least expect it.

We remember the incident of the Christian man who was the only one saved from a wrecked vessel after a storm at sea. He found himself cast upon a little island, and by great effort got certain materials together and managed to make a little shelter from the equatorial storms. He waited day after day praying God to send a ship to succor him, and he used to go down to the shore of the little island and wave a signal, just a piece of his clothing, every time he saw a ship passing in the distance, but some way or another they never saw him. One day as he was cooking his dinner, he beheld a ship some distance away and hurried to the shore, earnestly praying that this time they might see and come to his relief. He waved frantically, but they went by, until at last the little vessel was almost lost to sight. Then turning to plod his way back to his little hut he was astonished to see that it had burst into flames. He had left some embers, and the wind had set the place on fire. Everything burned, and then when at last he stood there utterly distressed, not knowing where he would be able to gather sufficient material to build another shelter, to his amazement he saw that the vessel was headed right for the island. As they neared the shore they sent a little boat for him and took him on board. He asked, "Did you see my signal?" "Your signal!" they said; "Yes, we saw your smoke, and so we came to rescue you." God had answered prayer, but not at all in the way he expected it, and so, some day when we get home to heaven, we shall see that many of the prayers we thought God had not heard were answered in His own wonderful way.

In this connection, I do not doubt that the thought will come to many minds, "What of faith healing? May I not pray for the sick, and will they not be healed?" Yes, if it be His will. But sometimes it is not. However, many will say, "Our blessed Lord is 'the same yesterday, and to-day, and for ever' (Heb. 13:8), and when on earth He healed all the sick that came. Therefore, we are assured that when those who are sick cry to Him or call their brethren in to pray, they will be healed." Of course, He is an unchanging Saviour, but His methods are not always the same. When He was here on earth He raised the dead, but He is not raising the dead now. However, He is the same Jesus, and by and by when He returns, He will raise the dead and prove that His power is just the same. But now we have to wait upon Him in regard to questions of physical healing.

So in verse 16 we read, "If any man see his brother—referring to a child of God—sin a sin which is not unto death, he shall ask, and he shall give him life for them that sin not unto death." The implication clearly is that sometimes—not always, but sometimes—sickness comes to children of God as divine chastening, as a means of correction and discipline because of waywardness. Sometimes the discipline has the desired effect in the spiritual restoration of the one who had failed and the body is healed also, but at other times it does not seem to be the will of God to raise up the disciplined one and put him in the place of testing again, and so we read, "There is sin unto

death: I do not say that he shall pray for it." Of
course it is physical death that is in question. He
is not speaking of eternal death: he is not speaking of the soul, but of the death of the body under
divine discipline. I think the indefinite article in
this part of the verse might better be omitted. It
is not that there is some specific sin that always
results in death, but there is *sin unto death*.

Moses and Aaron sinned unto death when they
became angry with the children of Israel and
smote the rock in indignation, instead of speaking to it as they had been commanded, and the
Lord said, "Because ye believed Me not, to sanctify Me in the eyes of the children of Israel, therefore ye shall not bring this congregation into the
land which I have given them" (Num. 20: 12).
Now there came almost immediate restoration.
Moses besought the Lord that He would forgive
him and permit him to enter the land, but the
Lord said, "Speak no more unto Me of this matter." Moses had sinned unto death. If today
every time Christians got angry they sinned unto
death, how few of us would be here! I am afraid
every one of us, unless there are some exception-
ally sweet-dispositioned people here, would be at
home in heaven. God would not have trusted us
any longer. Why was He so severe with Moses?
Moses was one who spoke with God face to face,
and the greater the privilege the greater the responsibility. Do not forget that.

Turning to the New Testament, we find the Spirit of God was working in great power in the early Church, and among the professed converts were two, Ananias and Sapphira, upon whose eternal state we are not called to decide inasmuch as Scripture does not pronounce upon it. They sinned against the Holy Ghost in pretending to a devotedness that they did not possess, and when they were faced with the sin, they told a lie. The result was that first Ananias and then Sapphira his wife fell down dead. They had sinned unto death. If God were dealing with all Christians that way now, how many of us would be here? How many Christians are there who have never pretended to a devotedness that they did not possess? How many Christians are there who have never permitted others to think that they were holier than they really are? And is there a Christian here who has not sometimes so forgotten what should characterize the believer that he has been guilty of a lie? You say, "Oh, but we bitterly repented." But, you see, for Ananias and Sapphira there was no restoration to a place of trust and confidence on earth. They had sinned unto death when they pretended to be more spiritual than they were, and when they lied concerning it.

We find another incident in the First Corinthian epistle. There was a great deal of laxity and carelessness of behavior at Corinth when they gathered together to take what we call today the communion, to observe the Lord's Supper; and because of the laxity, because of the carelessness that marked them, the apostle by the Holy Spirit writes like this: "For this cause many are weak and sickly among you, and many sleep" (1 Cor. 11: 30), or are dead. Sleep is the term he uses throughout that letter for the believer's death. If every time a Christian took the bread and cup at the communion table carelessly God were to visit with temporal death, how often tragedy would follow the observance of the Lord's Supper! So we cannot say of any particular sin that it is *the* sin unto death, but we say rather that there is sin unto death. God gives His people opportunity after opportunity, but if at last they deliberately go on refusing obedience to His Word, He says, "Now I am going to take you home; I won't trust you in the world any longer. I will deal with you at the judgment-seat of Christ."

I can look back on my own childhood and remember a group of children playing in the evening, and by and by there would be a quarrel, for children so readily change from having a good time to fussing with one another. A mother would appear in the doorway calling one of her own, "Here, what does this mean? You behave yourself."

"Yes, Mother. I will try to do better."

"Well, if you don't, you will have to come in."

And in a little while there is a fuss again, and again angry voices raised. Once more Mother's voice, "You come inside."

"Oh, Mother, I forgot myself. We are in the midst of a game. I will promise to be good."

"Very well, but you be careful."

The game goes on, and then once more a fuss, and the mother's voice says, "Now you come in."

"But Mother——."

"Not another word; you come inside."

"But, Mother, I will try to behave myself."

"No, I can't trust you any more tonight; come inside."

When inside maybe something takes place that we had better not speak of.

So with God and His children down here in this world. He gives them so many chances, He is so wonderfully gracious; and after a failure they repent and say, "Now I have learned my lesson." Perhaps a little later the same thing occurs, and then God says, "Now I am going to lay My hand upon you." Perhaps there is a long siege of illness, and they have an opportunity to bring it all to God in sincere confession, but the Lord says, "You have sinned unto death; I am going to take you home."

I once knew a splendid young man who left his home in obedience to what he believed to be the call of God to engage in Christian work in a needy district. He had not been there long before a

proposition for a very good temporal position
came between him and the Lord. Then too the
young woman whom he desired to marry declared
that she would never marry a preacher, and so
he decided to take the position. He settled down,
made money, and got ahead, but inwardly was
always very unhappy. He knew that he had
sinned against the Lord because he had been
called to a different service. By and by tuber-
culosis laid hold of him. He gave up his position
and spent the earnings of years in a sanitarium,
where he lay flat on his back. I was near by,
and he sent for me and said, "My brother, I want
you to pray with me, but not that the Lord will
raise me up, unless He should make it very
clear to you that it is His will. I have been facing a great many things here lately. I see my
failure now as never before. I believe I have
sinned unto death." I looked to the Lord asking,
if it was His will, to lift him up, but if not, to
give him great joy in departing. Two weeks
later I saw him again and he said, "I will never
see you on earth again. I have had two very
wonderful weeks. The Lord has been very near
to me, but He has told me that He is going to
take me home, that I lost my opportunity, and
that inasmuch as I chose my own comfort instead
of His will He can't trust me here any more.
But, thank God, I am perfectly resigned to His
will. I am going home!" And, sure enough,

three days later he died. He had sinned unto death, and it was useless to pray for his healing, but he went home happy in Christ.

"All unrighteousness is sin. and there is sin not unto death." All unrighteousness is sin and is therefore distasteful to God, but there are certain circumstances that do not make conditions quite so serious as others.

In verses 18 to 21 we have the epitome of all that has gone before, and this section is divided into three parts. Each one is introduced by the expression, "We know." This word translated *know* really means *an inward knowledge,* not merely that we know because we have read it, have heard it, or because some one has told us, but we know because of an inward assurance that has come to us. So John says, "We know that whosoever is born of God sinneth not"—doth not practise sin. "But he that is begotten of God keepeth himself, and that wicked one toucheth him not." This is just another way of saying that the child of God, having received a new nature, even though he does fall into sin, has an Advocate with the Father, Jesus Christ the righteous, and the accuser of the brethren will not be permitted to lay one charge against him, for he is in the hands of his own Father who will deal with him about his failures.

And then in the next instance we read, "And we know that we are of God, and the whole world

lieth in wickedness." This is sometimes translated, "The whole world lieth in the wicked one."
Somebody may say, "What assumption for a
little group of Christian people in a great city to
say that they have the inward knowledge, the
absolute assurance, that they are of God, and
that the whole world lieth in the wicked one!"
Yes, it may seem like assumption to men who do
not know God, but there is a reality about it that
cannot be explained to the world.

Take a young Christian, for instance, who has
but lately come to Christ, who is faced by the
specious arguments of atheists, agnostics, and
other unbelievers. He finds that he is unable to
answer their questions, and they say, "Well, you
see we have riddled your notions and proven to you
that you are all wrong and that God never spoke
to men." I have seen these young believers look
them full in the face and say, "I cannot answer
you, but I *know* that I have passed from death
unto life." I have seen many a man who had
lived a life of sin, now transformed by grace
divine, and when people said, "Explain it," he
would say, "I can't explain it." "Well, then,"
they would say, "we can't believe, because it is
contrary to certain laws, and if you can't show
that it is in harmony with these laws, we have to
reject it as simply the notions of an overwrought
brain." "You may think me crazy if you will,"
would come the answer; "I cannot explain it. But

one thing I know, whereas I was blind now I see, whereas I was once the victim of sinful habits that were wrecking and ruining my life, now I have found liberty in Christ Jesus." Explain that if you can. Every believer as he walks with God has this blessed inward knowledge. The only believer who loses it is the one who is disobedient to God. He loses the sense of this hallowed assurance, but when he comes back to God, makes a frank confession of his failure and is restored, he has once more this blessed inward knowledge by the Holy Spirit.

Then we read, "And we know that the Son of God is come, and hath given us an understanding, that we may know Him that is true, and we are in Him that is true, even in His Son Jesus Christ. This is the true God, and eternal life." Of course John could speak from actual knowledge, for he had leaned upon the breast of the Lord, he had walked with Him for all those wonderful years, he had heard the message proceeding out of His mouth, and he had seen His works of power. You may say, "But we have no such evidence." True, but we know nevertheless, for He has revealed Himself to us in His blessed Word. Blessed relationship, divine life, the same life that is manifested in all its fulness in Christ, partaken of by every believer. So, "we are in Him that is true."

Having spoken of our Lord Jesus, John imme-

diately adds, "This is the true God, and eternal
life." Who is the true God? Jesus Christ our
Lord. "This is the true God, and eternal life."
Eternal life is seen personally in Christ and communicated by Christ to those who believe in Him.

Now we have the closing exhortation, and
though brief, what an important one it is! "Little
children, keep yourselves from idols." Anything
that comes in between your soul and the path
of obedience to God is an idol, and sometimes God
has to come and take these idols away from us
in a way that seems very hard, and we may even
charge Him with being cruel, but it is in order
that Christ may have His rightful place, that
our hearts may be entirely devoted to Him. "Thou
shalt have no other gods before Me." And mark,
of Jesus Christ we read, "This is the true God;"
therefore any god other than the God revealed in
Jesus Christ is just an idol. In Christ alone God
is fully made known.

The Second Epistle of John

"The elder unto the elect lady and her children, whom I love in the truth; and not I only, but also all they that have known the truth; for the truth's sake, which dwelleth in us, and shall be with us for ever. Grace be with you, mercy, and peace, from God the Father, and from the Lord Jesus Christ, the Son of the Father, in truth and love. I rejoiced greatly that I found of thy children walking in truth, as we have received a commandment from the Father. And now I beseech thee, lady, not as though I wrote a new commandment unto thee, but that which we had from the beginning, that we love one another. And this is love, that we walk after His commandments. This is the commandment, That, as ye have heard from the beginning, ye should walk in it. For many deceivers are entered into the world, who confess not that Jesus Christ is come in the flesh. This is a deceiver and an antichrist. Look to yourselves, that we lose not those things which we have wrought, but that we receive a full reward. Whosoever transgresseth, and abideth not in the doctrine of Christ, hath not God. He that abideth in the doctrine of Christ, he hath both the Father and the Son. If there come any unto you, and bring not this doctrine, receive him not into your house, neither bid him God speed: for he that biddeth him God speed is partaker of his evil deeds. Having many things to write unto you, I would not write with paper and ink: but I trust to come unto you, and speak face to face, that our joy may be full. The children of thy elect sister greet thee. Amen" (2 John).

John's second and third brief letters, while altogether different to the epistle of eternal life with which we have been occupied so long, are, nevertheless, of great importance, inasmuch as they bring before us guiding principles that have often been overlooked, but are needful indeed if the people of God would walk together so as to please our absent Lord.

John primarily deals, as we have seen, with truth concerning the family of God, even as Peter has to do chiefly with the government of God, and Paul with the Church of God. But in these last letters, written many years after both Paul and Peter had sealed their testimony with their blood, we get instruction regarding Church fellowship that we cannot afford to ignore, if fellowship is to be real.

In Second John a Christian lady is warned regarding false teachers, and thus we learn what our individual attitude toward all anti-Christian propagandists should be so long as the Church is in the place of testimony.

In Third John it is the very opposite. We learn through the apostle's instruction to Gaius what our behavior should ever be towards those who are lovers of Christ and who go forth proclaiming His truth.

These epistles are charming in their simplicity, and give us a wonderful insight into the heart of the venerable man who here speaks of himself rather as a presbyter, or elder, than as an apostle, even though we know he was that.

In this second letter John addresses himself to "the elect lady and her children, whom (he writes) I love in the truth; and not only I, but all those that have known the truth" (ver. 1). There is no reason to suppose that the elect lady is the Church, as some have thought, nor yet that we should read, "the Lady Electa," as others have suggested. The elect lady was evidently a Christian matron who, with her children, adorned the doctrine of Christ. In all probability she was one who had been blessed and helped through John's ministry. Now she has evidently written to him for advice as to how she would be expected to act when importuned to open her home to false teachers. Would Christian charity demand that courtesy and hospitality be shown even to these, or were there other responsibilities which must first be considered?

John's letter is clearly an answer to hers. He emphasizes faithfulness to the truth, "for the truth's sake, which dwelleth in us, and shall be with us forever."

In his salutation he invokes grace, mercy and peace from God the Father and from the Lord Jesus Christ, the Son of the Father, and this in truth and love. How full the title here! Men were teaching derogatory things concerning our Lord. The Spirit would give Him fullest honor and recognition.

John's heart had been gladdened by the good

report that had reached him of the ways of her
household: her children walked in the truth in
accordance with the commandment received from
the Father. Hers was a veritable Christian home
in the midst of an ungodly world. This commandment is that which had been made known "from
the beginning:" the revelation of the will of God
as given by our blessed Lord, that "we should
love one another." But this love is not to be
confounded with mere fleshly sentimentality.
"This is love that we walk after His commandments." Again he emphasizes the fact that he
speaks of nothing new (as was customary, and
is today, with deceivers), but he says, "That as
ye have heard from the beginning, ye should walk
in it."

As in his first epistle, this is the beginning of
Christianity. The Christian teaching is not in
process of evolution; it is not passing from one
stage to another as theologians and religious phil-
osophers devise new systems. It is "the faith
once for all delivered to the saints." That which
is new and not "from the beginning" is but a
deceit and a delusion.

Many had already come to consider themselves
as advanced, and gloried in being freed from the
dogmas of the past. It is of such he speaks when
he says, "For many deceivers are entered into the
world who confess not that Jesus Christ is come
in the flesh." He refers to those later known as

Doketic Gnostics, who denied the humanity of our Lord. According to them there was the appearance of a man—but only an appearance. It is this error that we saw combated in the opening verses of the first epistle. All such teachers the apostle brands as deceivers and antichrists. They were opposed to the Christ of God. Their denial of His Manhood marked them out as unsaved men, enemies of the truth of God. To traffic with these apostates in any way was dangerous, hence the admonition: "Look to yourselves that we lose not those things which we have wrought, but that we receive a full reward" (ver. 8). Real believers could not lose what God had bestowed in grace, but there was grave danger that they would deprive themselves of the rewards for faithfulness if they ever tampered with the errors that were being taught by these apostates.

The primary reference, beyond all doubt, is to the Gnostics of various sects, whether Cerinthian, who distinguished (as Eddyítes, New Thought teachers, and others do today) between the man Jesus and the divine Christ who, according to them, came to abide upon and indwell Jesus at His baptism, or Doketists, who denied the reality of His physical body and held that it was only an "appearance" by which the Christ manifested Himself to men. There were many widely divergent schools of thought among these errorists, but all agreed in rejecting Christ's vicarious sacrifice for sin upon the cross. All alike would rob the believer of the great foundation truths upon which the soul's peace rests. They all prated of progress in the revelation of divine mysteries, but the apostle condemns all such haughty claims as he solemnly declares: "Whosoever goeth beyond, and continueth not in the teaching of Christ hath not God. He that continueth in the teaching of Christ he hath both the Father and the Son" (ver. 9).

He certainly has not in view real believers in our blessed Lord who may not see eye to eye with others regarding certain doctrinal subtilties, but the teachers thus described are not Christians at all. They have therefore no claim whatever upon the sympathetic co-operation of the people of God. So to this elect lady John says, "If there come any unto you, and bring not this teaching, receive him not into your house, neither greet him: for he that greeteth him is sharer in his evil deeds." This is clear enough, and for the subject heart needs no elucidation. It positively forbids a Christian to show any fellowship whatever with a teacher of soul-destroying error. Such have no title to the hospitality of believers who owe everything for eternity to the Saviour whom these apostates blaspheme.

The closing verses are beautiful in their simplicity, but require no comment.

The Third Epistle of John

"The elder unto the well-beloved Gaius, whom I love in the truth. Beloved, I wish above all things that thou mayest prosper and be in health, even as thy soul prospereth. For I rejoiced greatly, when the brethren came and testified of the truth that is in thee, even as thou walkest in the truth. I have no greater joy than to hear that my children walk in truth. Beloved, thou doest faithfully whatsoever thou doest to the brethren, and to strangers; which have borne witness of thy charity before the church: whom if thou bring forward on their journey after a godly sort, thou shalt do well: because that for His name's sake they went forth, taking nothing of the Gentiles. We therefore ought to receive such, that we might be fellow-helpers to the truth. I wrote unto the church: but Diotrephes, who loveth to have the preeminence among them, receiveth us not. Wherefore, if I come, I will remember his deeds which he doeth, prating against us with malicious words: and not content therewith, neither doth he himself receive the brethren, and forbiddeth them that would, and casteth them out of the church. Beloved, follow not that which is evil, but that which is good. He that doeth good is of God: but he that doeth evil hath not seen God. Demetrius hath good report of all men, and of the truth itself: yea, and we also bear record; and ye know that our record is true. I had many things to write, but I will not with ink and pen write unto thee: but I trust I shall shortly see thee, and we shall speak face to face. Peace be to thee. Our friends salute thee. Greet the friends by name" (3 John).

Third John is the correlative of Second John. In this letter we learn the breadth of Christian

fellowship, and in it narrow ecclesiasticism is
sharply rebuked.

In this case the apostle addresses Gaius, a
brother in the Lord, honored for his large-heart-
edness, whose home was ever open to properly
accredited preachers.   To him John expresses the
pious wish that he may prosper and be in health
as his soul prospers.   There was no doubt of the
latter condition.   But a weak body is often the
dwelling of a happy and prosperous soul.

Travelling brethren had reported to the aged
apostle the graciousness of Gaius and his walk
in the truth.   He was possibly a convert of John's,
as seems implied in the words, "I have no greater
joy than to hear that my children walk in truth."

Then he adds, "Beloved, thou doest faithfully
whatsoever thou doest to the brethren, even to
strangers; which have borne witness of thy love
before the Church: whom if thou bring forward
on their journey after a godly sort, thou shalt do
well: because for His name's sake they went
forth, taking nothing of the Gentiles."   What a
side-light this throws upon conditions in the early
Church! As the itinerating evangelists and teachers went about they were graciously entertained
by such as Gaius and helped on their way.   They
did not look to the world for sustenance.   They
recognized the fact that the Lord's work should
be supported by the Lord's people.   Thus they
were happily independent of the heathen to whom

they ministered, and so had a rightful claim upon the sympathetic help of fellow-believers. "We therefore *ought* to receive such that we might be fellow-helpers to the truth." All might not be gifted as preachers or teachers, but all could help those who were, and thus keep them independent of the world, but dependent upon God.

What a contrast this delightful Christian simplicity is to the unholy and utterly un-Christian financial methods of many today who are presumably attempting to follow in the steps of these first century workers! High-pressure efforts to squeeze money out of Christ-rejecters and even carnal Christians is thoroughly opposed to the grace of the gospel.

On the other hand Christians need often to be reminded that "we ought" to further the gospel by supporting to the best of our ability men approved by the truth they carry, as they launch out in dependence upon the Lord Himself.

From verses 9 and 10 we learn that already men had arisen in the churches who were of a narrow sectarian spirit, men of hard, rigid ecclesiastical views who despised these "free lances," as they might have termed them, and who desired to recognize only those who were of their particular stripe. John had evidently written to the church where Gaius was locally connected commending an itinerant named Demetrius, but he says, "Diotrephes, who loveth to have

the pre-eminence among them, receiveth us not."
He rejected Demetrius, and, in rejecting him he
was rejecting the apostle who endorsed him.
"Wherefore when I come," John continues, "I will
remember his deeds which he doeth, prating
against us with malicious words: and not content
therewith, neither doth he himself receive the
brethren, and forbiddeth them that would, and
casteth them out of the church."   Diotrephes was
the sample ecclesiastic to whom church order
meant more than love to Christ's sheep.   "He followeth not with us," would be his slogan, "therefore we cannot receive his ministry, nor show
him fellowship!"   Unhappily, the spiritual des-
cendants of Diotrephes are many.   They may be
found not only in the great denominations but in
the humblest Christian assemblies, self-seeking,
self-important, self-elected "bishops" and "over-
seers," lording it over their brethren and arrogat-
ing to themselves the right to say who may or may
not be recognized.   And woe unto any who opposes their pretentious *ipse dixit!*

John himself, an inspired apostle, had no fear
of the anathema of Diotrephes, but many a hum-
bler worker has been utterly discouraged and
turned aside by the presumptuousness of men of
similar spirit.   To such the message comes: "Beloved, follow not that which is evil, but that which
is good.   He that doeth good is of God (whether
approved by Diotrephes or not), and he that doeth

evil (whatsoever his ecclesiastical standing) hath not seen God" (ver. 11).

It is evident that the servant who had been so ruthlessly barred out by this self-elected leader is the man named in verse 12. "Demetrius hath good report of all men, and of the truth itself: yea, and we also bear witness, and ye know that our witness is true." But it matters nothing to the rigid advocates of a pseudo-church-order that a man is honored of God, that he proclaims the truth, that his walk is blameless, that many can testify to his devotedness and his piety, as also to the spirituality and helpfulness of his ministry —if "he followeth not with us" he must be treated as a publican and a sinner, or rejected as though he were a blasphemer. How shocking it all is, and what an insult to the Head of the Church and to the Holy Spirit of God!

How aptly these two epistles thus counterbalance each other: the one testifying against fellowship with apostasy, the other inculcating fellowship in the truth.

The closing verses here again are too plain to need any comment, but they testify to the freedom of communion between the venerable apostle and his friends in Christ.

Part Two

THE EPISTLE OF JUDE

PREFATORY NOTE

THE version used throughout this exposition is that of J. N. DARBY, and is used in preference to the commonly received translations, both *Authorized* and *Revised*, because of its close adherence in several places to the actual wording of the *Original*—though, in a few instances, this makes somewhat awkward English.

The exposition itself is by no means exhaustive, but it is hoped it may be suggestive and helpful, especially to such as are bewildered and endangered by the evils of our day, so plainly and forcibly depicted by Jude in the apostolic period.

It should be cause for thankfulness that, so far as error or heterodoxy is concerned, "there is nothing new under the sun." Every form of evil teaching now current was exposed by inspired writers in apostolic days. Therefore the need to contend earnestly for the faith once for all delivered—refusing all innovations, as of man or of Satan.

H. A. I.

EXPOSITION OF
THE EPISTLE OF JUDE

THE SALUTATION

"Jude, bondman of Jesus Christ, and brother of James, to the called ones, beloved in God [the] Father, and preserved in Jesus Christ: mercy to you, and peace and love be multiplied" (vers. 1, 2).

THERE seems no good reason to doubt, and every reason to believe, that the writer of this solemn yet comforting letter is the "Judas, the brother of James," mentioned in the list of the apostles, as given twice by Luke (Luke 6: 16; Acts 1: 13), but who is called by Matthew "Lebbeus, whose surname was Thaddeus" (Matt. 10: 3), and by Mark simply Thaddeus (Mark 3: 18). John distinguishes him in a special way by speaking of him as "Judas, not Iscariot" (John 14: 22). It is evident, from the way Paul writes of this James, the son of Alpheus, that he was a very near relation, according to the flesh, to our Saviour, the Lord Jesus. After mentioning his first interview with Peter, he says: "But other of the apostles saw I none, save James the Lord's brother" (Gal 1: 19). James the Great, the son of Zebedee, had met a martyr's death earlier than the visit here referred

to; consequently it becomes plain that James the
Less is meant. The term "the Lord's brother" does
not necessarily mean all that it would, had the epistle been written in our language; still it implies
very close relationship.　　Lot is called Abram's
brother, when actually he was his nephew.　Yet
even so, had Jude been desirous of making a fair
show in the flesh, he who was so closely related to
the Lord as man, would not have written of himself
as he does here, "Jude, *bondman* of Jesus Christ."
He had known Christ after the flesh; had been
linked up with Him by ties of kindred common to
few; but he knows Him so no more.　Gladly he
owns Him as God's anointed, his Lord and Master.
Another writing of him might, out of courtesy,
have used the same term as Paul applied to Jude's
brother; but writing of himself, he is simply the
"slave of Jesus Christ."　James speaks of himself
in the same way—"a bondman of God and of the
Lord Jesus Christ" (Jas. 1: 1).

What a withering rebuke are these two lovely
examples of devotion to Christ to those who thoughtlessly speak or write of "our brother Jesus," or
use similar terms, all calculated to detract from the
glory of Him who, once a lowly man in this scene
of His humiliation, is now, as man, by God exalted
to be a Prince and a Saviour, made, in resurrection,
both Lord and Christ.　His own words to His disciples, after performing the lowly work of washing their feet, were, "Ye call Me Master and Lord:
and *ye say well;* for so I am!" (John 13 : 13).　How
abhorrent is the pride that leads some to-day to

call themselves "Christadelphians" (Christ's brothers), as though He were—what indeed they believe
—but a creature like themselves !

True it is that in infinite grace having been, as
the Captain of our salvation, made perfect through
suffering (now crowned with glory and honor), "He
is not ashamed to call [us] brethren, saying, I will
declare thy name unto my brethren" (Heb. 2 : 11,
12). But this is a very different thing from calling
Him " Brother," or speaking of ourselves as His
brothers. If any object to this, let them search the
Scriptures; both those portions which portray His
walk on earth and those parts which present Him
in resurrection, and see if any ever so spoke of or
to Him. James and Jude, who might be thought
to have a good right so to do, scrupulously avoid
such familiarity, and own themselves His bondmen,
or slaves. And this is made all the more prominent
in Jude's letter, as he immediately adds, for the
purpose of identification, " brother of James."

He addresses himself to "the called ones" of
God. It is a common title of those whom grace
has saved. The Lord's words to His disciples
while on earth were: "Ye have not chosen Me, but
I have chosen you" (John 15 : 16); and some ac-
counted it a hard saying, when He declared, "Therefore said I unto you, that no man can come unto
Me, except it were given unto him of my Father"
(John 6 : 65). All such are called by His grace, as
was Paul (Gal. 1: 15), and thus attracted to Christ
from a world that lieth in the wicked one. Unspeakably great is the favor thus conferred. For

who is it He calls? Those who have some goodness to plead?—some merit to commend? No;
but those who know themselves utterly vile and
corrupt, and own their lost estate. All such are
"called unto the fellowship of His Son." "And
whom He called, them He also justified: and whom
He justified, them He also glorified" (1 Cor. 1 : 9;
Rom. 8 : 30). There can be no failure here. He
who called has justified, and will have every called
one in the glory for eternity.

Such are "beloved of God the Father." The *A.
Ver.* reads, "sanctified," but editors generally favor
the other word. Both are true; but it is to our place
in the affections of the Father that we are here
directed. Would we know the measure of that love?
Our Lord has Himself declared it, for He said,
when addressing His Father on that last night ere
He was crucified, "The glory which Thou gavest
Me I have given them; that they may be one, even
as We are one: I in them, and Thou in Me, that they
may be made perfect in one; and that the world
may know that Thou hast sent Me, and *hast loved
them as Thou hast loved Me*" (John 17: 22, 23). Nothing less than this is the measure of the Father's
love to every child of grace. There are no degrees
in His affections for them. The feeblest and the
strongest are alike "beloved of God the Father"
as truly as His Son is the Beloved of His heart.

From this flows our preservation—"Preserved in
Jesus Christ." Whatever may be the difficulties of
the way, however great the trial of our faith, in
this love of God we are preserved by the One who

has saved us. He it is who, "having loved His own
which are in the world, loves them to the end."
Were it not for His preserving grace not one saint
would persevere; but "He is able to save evermore
all who come unto God by Him, seeing that He ever
liveth to make intercession for them." Here is no
ground for self-confidence, or fleshly elation; but
such grace calls for reverent and adoring gratitude,
and a walk that corresponds to the loving-kindness
thus lavished on creatures so unworthy.

Jude uses a different greeting from that of the
other apostles. It is not "grace and peace," nor
yet "grace, mercy, and peace," which he invokes
upon the saints; but "mercy to you, and peace and
love be multiplied." They were already in the enjoyment of these precious things; he would have
them abundantly increased, and thus their souls
filled with holy joy.

Mercy each saint will need all along the way,
while passing through a world like this. It necessarily implies failure on the part of its object.
Peace is his portion while abiding in Christ, who
has said, "Peace I leave with you, my peace I give
unto you: not as the world giveth, give I unto you.
Let not your heart be troubled, neither let it be
afraid" (John 14 : 27). In the enjoyment of that
peace the soul can pass quietly on its way amid all
the strife of tongues and the confusion of the evil
day, resting in Him who is over all, and who "sit-
teth o'er the water-floods."

Love is the outflow of the new life. *God is love;*
and the divine nature in the believer, which is

from God, cannot but produce love; though this is very different from mere sentimentality, as the epistle goes on to show. "Love in the truth" is that which is according to God.

Abundant is the provision for each tried saint who has to meet the soul's enemy in a world of iniquity and corruption. If mercy, peace and love are ever lacking, it bespeaks, not a stinted supply of grace, but a failure to enter into what is freely bestowed upon all who receive with thanksgiving what our God so delights to give. He never casts a trusting, honest soul upon its own resources, but has pledged Himself to meet every need according to His riches in glory, through Christ Jesus. "Let us therefore come boldly unto the throne of grace, that we may obtain mercy, and find grace to help in time of need" (Heb. 4 : 16). Never will that time of need be over until we reach that scene where strife and warfare are past for ever.

"THE FAITH ONCE FOR ALL DELIVERED."

"Beloved, using all diligence to write to you of our common salvation, I have been obliged to write you, exhorting [you] to contend earnestly for the faith once delivered to the saints" (ver. 3).

BORNE along by the Spirit, Jude sat down to write. His own heart was filled with the joy of God's salvation; and as he put pen to parchment, he would have been glad to write of this salvation common to every saint. But verbal inspiration, however derided by unbelieving men, is ever affirmed in Scripture. So here the apostle is not left to himself as to the form or subject of his letter. The same Holy Spirit who caused him to give all diligence to write, directed his mind as to the theme he must dwell upon. Not the common salvation, precious as that is, was to be his line. A note of *warning* and *exhortation* it was, that the Lord would have him give. Therefore he writes to urge earnest contending for the faith already delivered, and that once for all. For the force of the word "once" is such as to debar all thought of repetition.

The faith here is not faith by which we lay hold of the salvation of God. It is the truth as to that salvation, with all that accompanies it. This abiding faith has been given never to be added to. No new revelations will be vouchsafed to complete the truth given by divine inspiration through the apostles of our Lord and Saviour Jesus Christ. Jude, as John, turns the saints back to "that which was from the beginning."

Evolution in theology there may be, for theology is simply the reasoning of man's mind as to the things of God. But evolution in regard to the truth, the faith once for all delivered, there is none. God has given His last word on the subject. For this we are called to contend.

It will be seen at once how this simple expression shuts out all the pretentious claims of new prophets, seers and revelators. Impious are the claims of latter-day enthusiasts who make bold to declare themselves sent of God to add unto His words. Be the signs and wonders that accompany such pretensions as remarkable as those of the Antichrist yet to come, the simple-hearted believer turns away from them all, and exclaims with holy confidence, "The faith has been once for all made known. Neither assumption nor miracle shall induce me to accept any additions to it."

It was for lack of this that in the last century so many thousands of the unwary were attracted and ensnared by the specious claims of Mormonism, which even yet, though in its decadence, numbers its converts by hundreds yearly. Angelic agencies and mystic plates—if all said about them were true, instead of palpably false—still would authenticate nothing. The faith once delivered needs neither angelic nor human additions. It is perfect and complete; and the man of God will refuse all other and newer revelations.

To the apostle Paul it was given to complete the Word of God. He was the chosen servant to whom the mysteries hidden from past ages were made known (Col. 1: 24–27). Having thus completed the outline of divine teaching, he can write, "Though we, or an angel from heaven, preach any other gospel unto you than that which we have preached unto you, let him be accursed " (Gal. 1 : 8).

Jude adds no new doctrine to what had already been set forth, but exhorts those who had received so sacred a deposit, to contend earnestly for it; even as John, in the Revelation, sets forth no additional line of teaching, but shows what the outcome is to be in regard to the conflict between truth and error, carried on so long.

It will be seen at once how fitting it is, therefore, that Jude's letter should be so placed in our Bibles as to form a preface to the book of Revelation; for such indeed it is. He gives a graphic and solemn picture of the evils (already springing up among the saints in those early days), which in Revelation are portrayed in all their hideous development.

That the second letter of Peter bears a close resemblance in many particulars to that of Jude is apparent to all careful readers: so much so that some, who never look below the surface, have surmised that one might be but an imperfect copy of the other. To the spiritually-minded there are, however, marked differences despite the striking similarity. Peter warns of false teachers, corrupting those who are not established in the truth. It is false doctrine, damnable heresies, which, if not refused, will bring upon the recipients of them swift destruction. But Jude has especially before him the ungodliness that results from the giving up of the truth. The grace of God turned into lasciviousness is that which he warns against.

Men may belittle sound doctrine, and ridicule as an antiquated notion that a system of belief is of any importance in regard to a man's behavior; but Scripture shows that there cannot be proper behavior apart from soundness in the faith. The couplet:

> "For modes of faith let graceless zealots fight;
> He can't be wrong whose life is in the right,"

expresses what is in the minds of many, but the life will never be in the right unless the truth of God is accepted and bears sway in the inward parts; therefore the need, in a day of abounding vagaries like the present, to heed such an exhortation as Jude here is inspired of the Holy Spirit to give.

The word is addressed, not to leaders alone, but to all the called in Jesus Christ. Each one is responsible, in a time of departure from the truth, to contend earnestly for all that God has revealed. Were the mass of Christians thus guarding the treasure committed to the whole Church, evil-workers and false teachers would be unable to obtain foothold; but it is because of the indifference of those who are content to be called the laity, that ungodly men are able to entrench themselves so strongly in that which bears the name of the Church.

To the saints as a whole the faith was delivered. To such the exhortation is addressed to contend earnestly for it. The believer is thus viewed in his soldier character: he is called upon to fight for what is in God's sight of such prime importance. As a Shammah, defending a patch of lentils, the food of God's people (2 Sam. 23:11, 12), so the Christian should boldly defend the truth against all enemies.

It is well to remember that it is one thing to contend; quite another, to be contentious. "The servant of the Lord must not strive; but be gentle unto all men, apt to teach, patient; in meekness instructing those that oppose themselves; if God peradventure will give them repentance to the acknowledging of the truth; and that they may recover themselves out of the snare of the devil, who are taken captive by him at his will" (2 Tim. 2: 24–26). These verses indicate the spirit that is to characterize the one who would contend for the truth.

Firmly, yet with tender compassion for those being led astray, he is to stand for all that God has revealed. When a bad, carnal spirit takes possession of one, he is powerless to help or bless others. And it should ever be remembered that in contending for the faith, the soul of the sinner has to be thought of likewise. It is not enough to uphold the doctrines of Christ, the behavior must command the truth which the lips proclaim. The phrase in Eph. 4: 15, translated "speaking the truth in love," has been literally rendered, "*truthing* in love." We do not have the participle form of the word in English, as in Greek; consequently it is awkward to so express it; but it gives the exact meaning. It is far more than speaking the truth that is in question. It is the truth lived out in all our ways. Unless this be characteristic of the one who contends for the faith of God's elect, the utterances of his lips will be but vain.

CLANDESTINE WORKERS.

"For certain men have got in unnoticed, they who were marked out beforehand to this sentence ; ungodly [persons], turning the grace of our God into dissoluteness, and denying our only Master and Lord Jesus Christ " (ver. 4).

FROM the days of Simon Magus to the present it has ever been the object of Satan to secretly introduce evil workers into the assemblies of the saints of God, that thus the simple and the unwary may be deceived and led astray. Nor have men been wanting in all ages who would stoop to do so nefarious a business.

The truth of God, if not submitted to, has a hardening effect upon the one who is familiar with it. To trifle with what God has revealed is an affront to Himself, which must have dire consequences. Such would seem to be the state of the men against whom Jude here warns the people of God. They are men who have a mental acquaintance with the truth, but whose ways are not in accordance with that which they profess to hold. Clandestinely they have slipped into the assemblies of the saints, but they are not unknown to God, though they have managed to deceive His people. Before, of old, they were marked out to this judgment. "Ordained" is too strong a word here, and fails to give the true thought. Far be it from the Holy One to ordain any man to acts of impiety and ways of deceit! But He had of old marked them out, declaring by His servants that such men should arise, giving their characteristics clearly, so that they might readily be recognized—their end was judgment. This too He had pointed out.

They are described as ungodly men. This term "ungodly" is used five times in the epistle, the other four instances occurring in the quotation from Enoch. It means refusing subjection to God, acting independently of and in opposition to God. For the ungodly Christ died—all men in their sins are so called. But here we have those who by profession are delivered from their sins, but who actually are still in them, and secretly turning others into their own iniquitous ways.

The grace of God has neither reached their souls nor controlled their consciences. They make that very grace an occasion for lasciviousness of speech and life. Such evil-workers have abounded in all periods since the gospel was made known. But, be it noted, the remedy is never, in Scripture, legality, but a bowing to the truth of man's need of that very grace he has been misusing. The sinner who judges himself before God and finds his need met in that wondrous provision of grace will not, if walking with Him, be found turning such unmerited favor into dissoluteness. It is the unrepentant professor, who has never seen himself in the light of God's holiness, who is here referred to.

Some may ask, In what way do men turn the grace of God into lasciviousness? The answer undoubtedly is by going on in their own ways, gratifying the lusts of the flesh, while professing to believe in the grace that does not impute sin to the justified soul. This is what has been well-named Antinomianism. Often those have been charged with holding it who with all their hearts abhor it, and who, subdued by grace, gladly seek to render willing service to Him whose loving-kindness has saved them without merit of their own. Such are the very opposite to those here presented, who know not in reality the grace of which they prate.

These deny our only Master (*A. V.* reads Lord God) and our Lord Jesus Christ. It is not to be supposed that they definitely deny Him at all times with their lips. Often they are found professing to know Him, but denying Him by their works.

One needs not to look far to find men of this stamp. Christendom to-day abounds with them. In the seats of honor, and also among the so-called laity, they " feed themselves without fear," professing allegiance to Christ while ignoring His word and even treating with contempt and assumed superiority the Sacred Writings. Nothing is too holy for their profane reasonings to set aside. " From such turn away."

To no time in the past history of the Church have Jude's words applied with greater force than in the present latitudinarian age. In Romanism, emissaries make strenuous efforts to allure the unwary by presenting a softened, subdued Catholicism to non-Catholics ; they emphasize largely whatever is really Scriptural, or ethically and esthetically lovely in the teachings of the Papacy, and carefully cover the grosser and more disgusting

dogmas and practices of that apostate church.*
In Protestantism, the boldest infidelity and skep-
ticism are proclaimed from thousands of pulpits;
and minor sects of all shades of heterodoxy are
everywhere busy spreading their pernicious and
soul-destroying errors; hence the man of God needs
to be alert and vigilant—devotedly to stand for the
faith once for all delivered to the saints.

A mock charity would say that it makes little
difference what a man believes if he live well and
be sincere. The soul subject to Scripture knows
that the gospel alone is "the power of God unto
salvation to every one that believeth," and he remembers that the Holy Spirit has pronounced
solemn curses against any, even an angel from
heaven, who brings a different gospel—which is not
another.

The fact is that well-living, according to the
divine standard of holiness and uprightness, is a
delusion and an impossibility, apart from the sanc-
tifying power of the truth of God. Hence it will
be found that where false teaching prevails, ungodliness abounds, as witness the wretchedly low
standard of Christian living maintained by Roman-
ists; the worldliness of professors of the latitudi-

---

* It will be noticed that the Paulists, an order of missionary
priests devoted to the perversion of Protestants, always put to the
fore such fundamental doctrines as the Trinity, the deity of Christ,
etc., but rarely touch upon those offensive teachings of that corrupt church which for so long drugged the nations with the wine
of her fornication. Thus the simple are enticed, and walk into
Babylon's gates like sheep going to the slaughter.

narian type, the over-weening pride, coupled with an exceedingly poor imitation of godliness, that characterizes those professing a "second blessing" of absolute holiness—all alike evidence the baneful effects of teaching contrary to the faith of God's elect.

Indifference to evil teaching, and genuine love for Christ and His truth cannot co-exist in the same breast. Neutrality in such a case is a crime against the Lord who has redeemed us to Himself.

Destruction of Apostates

"But I would put you in remembrance, you who once knew all things, that the Lord, having saved a people out of the land of Egypt, in the second place destroyed those who had not believed. And angels who had not kept their original estate, but had abandoned their own dwelling, He keeps in eternal chains, under gloomy darkness, to the judgment of the great day; as Sodom and Gomorrha, and the cities around them, committing greedily fornication, in like manner with them, and going after other flesh, lie there as an example, undergoing the judgment of eternal fire" (vers. 5-7).

WHEN the saint of God dwells on the end awaiting all apostates from the truth, who persist in their impious doctrines and unholy practices, all bitterness toward them must of necessity be banished from the heart. They may seem to ride now on a crest of popular appreciation and support, but "their feet shall slide in due time," for they are set in slippery places, and shall soon be cast down to destruction (Ps. 73).

This is the solemn lesson taught by the unbelieving host who fell in the wilderness. They started out well—all were baptized unto Moses in the cloud and in the sea—all drank the same spiritual drink and ate the same spiritual food, but unbelief manifested itself when the time of testing came. Murmuring, idolatry, and the gainsaying of Korah (of which particular note is taken in this epistle farther down), told out the true state of many who sang with exultation on the banks of the Red Sea. Kadesh-Barnea, the place of opportun-

ity, became but the memorial of lack of faith; and
though once saved out of Egypt, they were destroyed in the wilderness because of having apostatized from the living God.

In the same way had the *Nephilim* (the fallen
ones) been dealt with long before. Though created
as sinless angels of God, they, like Lucifer, the son
of the morning, bartered the realms of bliss for selfish ends. Keeping not the glorious estate in which
they were created, they abandoned their holy abode,
and are now kept "in eternal chains, under gloomy
darkness," awaiting the judgment of the great day.

Whether the apostle is here referring to the
"sons of God" of Gen. 6 has been a mooted question
throughout the Christian centuries. That the beings there referred to could possibly be angels has
been scouted by many spiritually-minded teachers,
who see in "the sons of God" simply the seed of
Seth, and in "the daughters of men" the maidens of
the line of Cain. Others, equally deserving to be
heard, identify the sons of God of the book of Job
with those of Genesis; and, accepting the passage
before us as the divine commentary on the solemn
scene of apostasy described as the precursor of the
flood, believe they here learn the judgment of the
fallen ones whose sin is there delineated.

It must be admitted that the following verse in
Jude seems to corroborate this latter view. "*As*
Sodom and Gomorrha, and the cities around them,
committing greedily fornication, *in like manner with*
them," would appear to indicate a close relationship between the sin of these cities and that of the

angels referred to.* At any rate, they were one in this, that both angels and the men of the plain fell into grievous sin through unbelief, and were punished accordingly.

It was light rejected that paved the way for the unprintable enormities of the inhabitants of the cities of the plain, who are now set forth as an example, suffering, or undergoing, the vengeance of eternal fire.

Nothing can be more solemn than this. Long ages have elapsed since fire from heaven destroyed those cities, reeking with moral pestilence. But the guilty apostates of that far-distant day are at this moment still suffering the judgment of God because of their wicked deeds. They are with the once rich man of Luke 16, tormented in the flames of hades, while waiting for the awful hour when, as Rev. 20: 14 declares, "death and hades shall be cast into the lake of fire!

This passage, carefully considered, will throw a

---

* The comments of W. Kelly, C. E. Stuart, W. Scott, and others, may be consulted as favoring this view. Both J. N. Darby and F. W. Grant are, perhaps wisely, non-committal. The same is true of C. H. Mackintosh. W. Lincoln in "Typical Foreshadowings," opposes it with vigor.

.   .   .   .   .   .

Since writing the above, I have come across the following from the pen of J. N. D., in " Notes and Comments," Vol. I., page 73: "Jude and Peter seem to make the *B'ney ha-Elohim* (sons of God) the angels; but God effaced all this in the Deluge, and so may we; but the Titans and mighty men, heroes, find the origin of their traditions here.

"I have little doubt this is purposely obscure, but the language here, in itself, tends to the thought that *B'ney Elohim* were not of the race of *Ha-Adam* (man)."

lurid light on a scripture which, perverted from its proper meaning, has become a favorite one of late years with those who deny the eternal conscious punishment of the wicked, holding out instead the delusive dream of annihilation: I refer to Mal. 4: 1-3. "For, behold, the day cometh, that shall burn as an oven; and all the proud, yea, and all that do wickedly, shall be stubble: and the day that cometh shall burn them up, saith the Lord of hosts, that it shall leave them neither root nor branch. But unto you that fear my name shall the Sun of righteousness arise with healing in his wings; and ye shall go forth, and grow up as calves of the stall. And ye shall tread down the wicked; for they shall be ashes under the soles of your feet in the day that I shall do this, saith the Lord of hosts." This passage is looked upon by the annihilationist as one of his strongest proof-texts. Assuming that the passage is treating of the final judgment, he exclaims, "What could be clearer? If the wicked are burned up like stubble, if neither root nor branch is left remaining, must they not necessarily have utterly ceased to exist? Furthermore, if they become as ashes under the soles of the saints' feet, where is room for the awful thought of an immortal soul suffering endless judgment?"

The superficial thinker is apt to think such questions conclusive in favor of annihilation. But a more careful survey of the chapter makes manifest the fact that it has no reference to judgment after death; but the Holy Ghost is there describing the destruction of apostates at the coming of the

Lord to establish His kingdom; prior, therefore, to the Millennium of Rev. 20. It is the *bodies* of the wicked, not their souls, which are thus to become as ashes under the feet of triumphant Israel. Like stubble, they will be destroyed as with devouring fire, so that neither root nor branch shall remain. So it was in the day when Sodom and Gomorrah, and the surrounding cities, met their doom. Lot or Abraham might then have trodden down the wicked, who would have been ashes under the soles of their feet after the terrible conflagration. All had been burned up, root and branch. But were they then annihilated? Not so. Our Lord Jesus says, "It shall be more tolerable for Sodom and Gomorrah in the day of judgment" than for those who rejected His ministry when here on earth. The very men and women who were burned to ashes so long ago are to rise from the dead for judgment. Where are they now, and what is their condition? Are they wrapped in a dreamless slumber, waiting in unconsciousness, till the sounding of the trump of doom? Nay, the soul-sleeper and the annihilationist are both wrong. They "are set forth as an example, undergoing the judgment of eternal fire!"

Truly, "it is a fearful thing to fall into the hands of the living God." Judgment unsparing must be the portion of all who trifle with the grace shown in the Cross to guilty sinners. Better far never to have heard of Christ and His blood, than, having heard, to turn from the truth so earnestly pressed in the word of God, to the soul-destroying fables of these latter and last days, which are yearly reaping their harvests of lost souls.

Oh, to be awake to the solemnity of these things! "Knowing the terror of the Lord," cried the great apostle to the nations, "we persuade men." And it was the very same who wrote, "The love of Christ constraineth us." Man, energized by Satan, would divorce the two, making much of love, and deriding the thought of eternal retribution. The soul subject to Scripture remembers that "God is light" is as true as "God is love."

In turning from so solemn a theme, I add a word as to apostasy. It is only the Christless professor who thus sells his birthright for the devil's mess of pottage. God has said, "If any man draw back, My soul shall have no pleasure in him." But the Holy Ghost is careful to say of true believers, "We are not of them who draw back unto perdition; but of them that believe to the saving of the soul" (Heb. 10: 38, 39). It is only those who endure to the end who shall be finally saved; but all will endure, through grace divine, who are born of God. "Who is he that overcometh the world, but he that believeth that Jesus is the Son of God?" (1 John 5: 5).

IRREVERENT AND IRRATIONAL DESPISERS OF THE TRUTH

"Yet in like manner these dreamers also defile the flesh, and despise lordship, and speak railingly against dignities. But Michael the archangel, when disputing with the devil he reasoned about the body of Moses, did not dare to bring a railing judgment against [him], but said, The Lord rebuke thee. But these, whatever things they know not, they speak railingly against; but what even, as the irrational animals, they understand by mere nature, in these things they corrupt themselves" (vers. 8–10).

UNHOLY ways always accompany, and indeed spring from, unholy teachings. Hence we can easily understand the readiness with which apostates from the truth give themselves up to what is defiling and abominable. It is noticeable that present-day advocates of that insult to decency denominated "free love," are in large measure persons who have apostatized from a nominal Christianity, and now can tolerate, and even stand for, what they once would have abhorred. The loosening of the marriage tie, the prevalent evil of unscriptural divorce and all its train of iniquitous practices, find in modern latitudinarian thought and liberal theology earnest defenders. What would once have been rebuked, even by the world, is now pandered to by a Christless pulpit, and so men and women sustaining unholy relations are rocked to sleep in their sins and made comfortable with the vaporings of "filthy dreamers," while death, judgment and eternal punishment are fast hastening on! The rejection of the inspiration of the Bible places the law of God, as expressed in the ten words from Sinai, among the productions of the human mind, and therefore its code of morals may be spurned and a lower ethical system, more in keeping with present day conditions, substituted. Hence loose standards prevail where Scripture no longer speaks with authority: " They have rejected the word of the Lord, and what wisdom is in them ? "

Coupled with this new standard of morals, so opposed to the purity of Scripture, will be found a pride that brooks no bounds, and vaunts itself against every unseen power. Satan is no longer feared, but his very existence denied on the one hand, or his superhuman ability ridiculed on the other. How different was the behavior of Michael the archangel, who, when he disputed with the great adversary about the body of Moses, durst not rail, but said, " The Lord rebuke thee ! "

All kinds of ingenious theories have been advanced concerning the nature of this dispute; but as God Himself has not given us the particulars, it would seem useless to speculate. Moses appeared in body on the mount of transfiguration with Elijah. That the dispute may have had something to do with preserving his body from corruption in view of that wondrous occasion, seems likely * but beyond that, it is best not to give rein to the notions of the mind. When we know as we are known, this and

---

* Is it not more likely that *to prevent idolatry* the place of Moses' burial was hidden from Israel ? Because of idolatry, King Hezekiah destroyed the brazen serpent that Moses had made (2 Kings 18 : 4).

1 Cor. 15 : 50 shows that it could not be in his natural body that Moses appeared on the Mount in glory with the Lord.—[Ed.

all other mysteries will be solved in a scene where knowledge can no longer puff us up as here.

It is important to observe that we never read of archangels in Scripture. Men may so talk, but God's word never. The word occurs only in the singular. Michael (meaning, "who is [as] God") is *the* archangel. Gabriel, for instance, is never so called. Some have sought to identify Michael with the Son of God Himself. But as there is no word from the Holy Spirit that declares such an identity, it is unwise to theorize. In the writer's judgment the evidence is all the other way.

Michael appears in the book of Daniel as "the great prince that standeth for the children of thy [the prophet's] people;" that is, of Israel. In Revelation he appears as the leader of the angelic hosts driving Satan from the heavens when his days of accusing the brethren are ended. Here he is seen contending for the lawgiver's body; and in 1 Thess. 4 he seems to be a distinct being, whose voice (as Israel's prince) will be heard in connection with the shout of the Lord and the trump of God at our Saviour's coming to gather His redeemed to Himself in the air. It is noticeable that in Dan. 10. 13 he is called, by another angel, "Michael, one of the chief princes;" a title, it would seem, utterly inconsistent with Him who was known of old as "The Angel of the Covenant"—now as our Lord Jesus Christ, the Only-begotten Son of God.

It is solemn indeed to be told that so great a being "durst not" bring a railing accusation against the devil, while proud, haughty men, ignorant of God, of Satan, and of themselves, speak boldly against all that is high, and rail concerning things utterly beyond their comprehension.

Even in what they do understand they do not behave with propriety but, like natural brute beasts, they corrupt themselves, manifesting complete inability to curb their fleshly lusts; while, knowing no shame, they dare to rail against the admittedly unknowable, if a divine revelation be rejected. But, alas, this is the result of the deification of the human mind, the root-error of the so-called "New Thought," "Christian Science," and other "oppositions of science, falsely so-called."

Thus the harvest is fast ripening for judgment, and it becomes increasingly important that those who know God search His word and value His truth; remembering that perilous times have indeed come, when, if it were possible, Satan would deceive the very elect.

If some are kept from error and the evil practices resultant, it is only through the same grace that saves; even as the apostle tells the Thessalonians, after warning them of the energetic working of the mystery of lawlessness and the coming strong delusion: "But we ought to give thanks to God always for you, brethren beloved of the Lord, that God has chosen you from the beginning to salvation in sanctification of the Spirit and belief of the truth" (2 Thess. 2: 13). If any abide in the truth, it is owing to the fact that God himself has chosen them, and sustains them in their path. "Where is boasting then? It is excluded!"

THREE-FOLD APOSTASY

"Woe to them! because they have gone in the way of Cain, and given themselves up to the error of Balaam for reward, and perished in the gainsaying of Core [Korah]" (ver. 11).

Three-fold is the apostasy here treated of. I purpose to take up the distinct phases, brought here to our notice so solemnly, under three separate heads, and so direct attention first to

"The Way of Cain."

Strictly speaking there are but two religions in the world;*—the true, that of God's appointing; the false, the product of man's own mind. The first is the religion of faith; the second that of credulity or superstition, in whatever form it may appear.

In the beginning God made known to guilty man the truth that death and judgment were his rightful portion, only to be averted by the sacrifice of the glorious Seed of the woman, who in the fulness of time should appear as the sinner's Saviour, bruising the serpent's head, though Himself wounded in the heel. This was the primeval revelation. In accordance therewith, faith taught those in whose souls grace had wrought, the propriety of approaching God, the Holy One, on the ground of sacrifice; each bleeding victim pointing on to Him who was to be made sin that guilty men might be delivered

---

* See a gospel volume, by the same writer, "The Only Two Religions, and Other Papers." Paper covers, 20 cts.; cloth, 50 cts. Same publishers.

from their sins and stand before the throne of the
Most High uncondemned. Therefore we read, "*By
faith* Abel offered unto God a more excellent sacrifice than Cain, by which he obtained witness that
he was righteous, God testifying of his gifts: and
by it, he being dead, yet speaketh" (Heb. 11: 4).
Mark, it was not by intuition, but by *faith*—through
a revelation apprehending the mind of God—Abel
offered. He brought that which told of a life for-
feited—a sinless substitute, whose vicarious death
could be placed over against the desert of the
guilty one. Of this the lamb out of the flock
speaks loudly, though he who offered it has long
been numbered with the dead in Christ.

This is the pith and marrow of the gospel "Christ
died for the ungodly." "He was wounded for our
transgressions; He was bruised for our iniquities;
the chastisement of our peace was upon Him, and
by His stripes we are healed." "It is the blood
that maketh an atonement for the soul." Everywhere in Scripture the same testimony is given, for
"without shedding of blood there is no remission."

Now this is exactly what, in principle, Cain denied. He brought an offering to God according to
the promptings of his own heart "deceitful above
all things and desperately wicked," as is the heart
of every natural man. His sacrifice seemed fair
and lovely: the fruits of the ground, wrung there-
from by toil and travail. But there was no recognition of the true character of sin and its desert.
God's sentence of death on account of sin is refused;
therefore no life is given, no blood is brought. This

is natural religion as opposed to what has been revealed. The fruits presented picture well man's
effort in all that is fairest in character-building, all
that is loveliest in human attainment—beautiful
indeed if the fruit of divine grace already known
in the soul—but of no avail whatever to meet the
claims of divine justice, to purge the conscience
and cleanse the soul from the stain of sin. It is
surely plain, then, that "the way of Cain" is a
most comprehensive title, embracing every form of
religious teaching, ceremony, or cult that ignores
the need of the vicarious atonement of our Lord
Jesus Christ.

Whether it be the substitution of rites and cere-
monies for simple faith in Him who died upon the
cross, as is so frequently the case in Romanist or
heathen communions; or whether it be the subtle
and refined speculations of modern religio-meta-
physical systems (denominated Theosophy, New
Thought, Christian Science, Rationalism, and so
on, *ad lib.*), which all tend to deify man in his own
estimation and free him from what is held to be
"the degrading thought" that he is *a sinner needing a Saviour ;*—all spring from one and the same
thing, the pride of the human heart, which substi-
tutes the notions of the unregenerate mind for the
revealed truth of the Word of God. All are but
different forms of the one common human religion
—the way of Cain—and can only lead their deluded
followers to share Cain's doom.

The vaunted New Theology of the day is as old
as the fallen creation. It was first pictured in the

fig-leaf garments of Adam and Eve; then crystal-ized, as it were, in the offering of Cain: and every sinner too proud to own his guilt and trust the atoning sacrifice of the Christ of God has been an adherent to it, whatever form his superstition may have taken.

Back to the way of Cain thousands are turning who once *professed* to have an interest in the blood of Christ. Counting that blood a common thing, as the blood of a mere martyr for righteousness' sake and liberty of conscience, they trample beneath their feet its *atoning* value and haughtily dare to approach the High and Lofty One that inhabiteth Eternity with the fruits and flowers of nature, boasting in what would be the occasion of their deepeet repentance if they had received the love of the truth that they might be saved.

So with readiness, refusing the ministry of the Holy Spirit, they give themselves up to the

"The Error of Balaam."

Of the false prophet who taught Balak to cast a stumbling-block before the people of Israel, we read three times in the New Testament. In a passage very nearly similar to the one before us, Peter writes of "the *way* of Balaam" (2 Pet. 2: 15). The glorified Christ, in the Apocalypse (2 : 14), speaks of "the *doctrine* of Balaam," and Jude, here, mentions his *error*. That the three are most intimately related is self-evident. Out of his errors sprang both his way and his doctrine. He was a striking example of those who suppose that the object of godliness is to make gain, and who consider it a right and proper thing that religion should be used to minister to one's personal advantage. Leo the Tenth was a true disciple of Balaam when he exclaimed to his cardinals, "What a profitable thing this myth about Jesus Christ has been to us!"* And every person, of whatever sect or system, or perchance outside of all such, has followed after the error of Balaam, who enters upon the dispensing of religious mysteries with a view to financial or other emolument.

Balaam's history, as recorded in the book of Numbers, is an intensely solemn one. He "loved the wages of unrighteousness." While professedly a prophet of God, he endeavored to prostitute his sacred office to the accumulation of wealth. At times, deterred by fear, again by a sense of the proprieties, he yet persists in the effort to either curse or seduce the people of God for his own advantage. He stands before us branded on the page of inspiration as one who, for temporary profit, would stifle his own convictions and lead astray those directed by him.

The same dreadful error is at the bottom of the vast majority of evil systems being at present propagated by zealous workers. Which of them would exist for a month if it were not for the baneful influence of gold? Try to imagine modern faddists giving freely what they profess to believe is divine; suffering uncomplainingly, in order to carry their

---

*How like Simon the magician of Acts 8: 18, 19.—[Ed.

false gospels to the ends of the earth; dying trium-
phantly to seal their testimony in blood, as did the
early Christians, and as do many godly and zealous
believers still.

Let the mind range o'er the whole host of heter-
odox sects : the golden spell of mammon is upon
nearly every one. And in all human systems, however orthodox outwardly, where the Word of truth
is departed from, the same potent spell assumes
control of preachers and teachers whose lips should
keep knowledge, and whose hearts should be free
from covetousness.

This it is that leads to the effort to please, not
God, but men. Smooth things are prophesied ;
truths offensive to ticklish ears are scarcely touched
upon, or altogether avoided, and all in order that
the purse-strings of the ungodly may be loosened,
and the ministry be made a profitable and honor-
able occupation.

Of old, Christ's servants went forth in simple dependence upon Himself, for His name's sake, "taking nothing of the Gentiles." Elisha-like, they
refused anything that looked like payment tendered
for the gift of God. Abraham-like, they would
not be enriched by Sodom's king. Peter-like, they
spurned the money of the unworthy that no evil
taint might be upon their ministry, nor a slave be
put upon the sinner's conscience. But it is far
otherwise with the popular apostles of a Christless
religion. Gehazi-like, they would run after every
healed Naaman and beg or demand a fee. Lot-
like, they pitch their tent towards, then build a

house in Sodom and under Sodom's patronage. Like Simon Magus, whose very name gives title to this most odious of all sins, they practise their simony unblushingly, and think indeed that the gift of God *can* be purchased with money. But the dark clouds of judgment are gathering overhead, and soon they shall learn, as Balaam did, the folly of pursuing so evil a way.

"The gainsaying of Korah"

is the last of this unholy trinity of apostasy. The way of Cain is false religion. The error of Balaam is false ministry. The gainsaying of Korah is false worship and rebellion against Christ's authority.

Korah was not a priest, neither were any of his rebellious company. They were Levites, whose business it was to attend to the outward service of the tabernacle. But lured on by pride they rose up against Moses and Aaron (typical of Christ as "the Apostle and High Priest of our confession"), and setting aside God's anointed, sought to force their way into His presence as priests to worship before Him without divine warrant or title. This is what is everywhere prevalent to-day. Independent and inflated with a sense of their own self-importance, vain men openly rebel against the authority of the Lord as Apostle and Priest, and dare to approach God as worshipers apart from Him, and ignore His claims. This is the kernel of Unitarianism, and the leaven that is fast permeating unbelieving Christendom. The cry that all men by nature are sons of God; that they need no mediating High Priest is heard on every hand, and will increase and spread as the end draws nearer.

Jude says that these apostates "perished in the gainsaying of Korah." He speaks of their doom as a settled thing. Just as sure as judgment overtook the dwellers in the tents of wickedness of old, when the earth opened her mouth and Korah and all his company went down alive into the pit, so shall the yawning gulf of woe receive in due time these insolent rebels against the Lord of glory, in the day when He, who has borne with their impiety so long in grace, shall arise to judgment.

It is precious to read in Num. 5 11, "Notwithstanding the sons of Korah died not." Linked as they were by natural ties to the proud rebel, they chose a different course, and their children are heard singing, in Ps. 84, "I had rather sit on the threshold of the house of the Lord than to dwell in the tents of wickedness." Happy indeed is it for all who are numbered in the same holy company, and who saved from going down to the pit, eschew the practices of all who go in the way of Cain, and run greedily after the error of Balaam for temporary reward, whose doom will be to perish in the gainsaying of Korah!

THE DIVINE INDICTMENT OF EVIL WORKERS

"These are spots in your love-feasts, feasting together [with you] without fear, pasturing themselves ; clouds without water, carried along by the winds ; autumnal trees, without fruit twice dead, rooted up ; raging waves of the sea, foaming out their own shame ; wandering stars, to whom has been reserved the gloom of darkness for eternity" (vers. 12, 13).

There is something unspeakably solemn in this severe indictment of those who, professedly followers of Christ and servants of God, really walk in a self-chosen path, and are elsewhere described as "enemies of the cross of Christ: whose end is destruction, whose God is their belly, and whose glory is in their shame, who mind earthly things" (Phil. 3: 18, 19). Be it carefully remembered that, throughout Jude's warning letter, the evil-workers referred to are not those who, outside the circle of profession, are confessedly the opponents of Christ and of the truth of God; but they are a self-seeking, worldly-minded, mammon-actuated class inside the nominal church, who make their profession of faith in the Lord Jesus a cover for their own selfish ends. They are often looked upon as leaders of Christian thought and champions of truth and righteousness. But underlying all they say and do, there is the open, or covert, denial of everything that really makes for godliness. To the heavenly calling they are strangers; hence their aim and object is to advance their own interests in this world. They dwell upon the earth. Pilgrimage in the scriptural sense they know not of. Their place and portion are in this scene, not up there, where Christ as Man glorified sits, rejected by earth, but accepted of heaven, at the right hand of God.

Metaphor after metaphor is used by the Holy Spirit to describe these false apostles and ministers of unrighteousness. Every phrase is important, and demands careful consideration.

" These are spots in your love-feasts." Perhaps, in place of "spots," it will be clearer if we read, "sunken, or hidden rocks." Such are these apostate teachers. Clearly-marked charted rocks are not of great danger, as a rule, to the mariner. It is those that are hidden, over whose jagged edges roll the deceitfully peaceful waters, that are most to be dreaded. Were these false guides to proclaim themselves publicly as opposed to what the godly hold sacred, their influence would be speedily nullified, save with a few whose senses have never been exercised to discern between good and evil. But, posing as advocates of the truth, soft-spoken and affable, with their good words and fair speeches they deceive the hearts of the simple.

The expression, "feasting themselves together [with you] without fear," shows how fully they have gained the confidence of the mass. Participating fearlessly in the most hallowed seasons of Christian communion, they never enter into the spirit of those happy expressions of love and fellowship, but observe the form, pretending to piety and devotion, while all the time looking but to their own interests, as the next expression strikingly emphasizes.

"Pasturing, or shepherding, *themselves*," in place of shepherding the flock of God—what could more vividly express the conception of the clerical position in the minds of many who trade upon its privileges. They who should feed the sheep and lambs of Christ's flock, fleece them instead, and look upon them as those whose place it is to contribute to their honor, wealth, and dignity. Scripture knows of no distinction between clergy and laity. All believers are God's *kleros**—His allotted portion. If of their own number there are those raised up to act as pastors, by guiding and caring for those weaker or less instructed, it is as doing a service to the Lord, the Chief Shepherd—"not for filthy lucre, but of a ready mind; neither as being lords over possessions (*kleros*, Gr.), but being en-samples to the flock" (1 Pet. 5 : 1-4).

To this single-eyed and true-hearted devotedness these deceitful workers are utter strangers. Their true characters are even more graphically depicted in the metaphors taken from nature that immediately follow.

"Clouds [they are] without water, carried along by the winds." Big with promise, pretentious and impressive, all knowledge and all mysteries seem to be in their keeping; but their utterances are a disappointment to any who know the mind of God as revealed in His word. In place of refreshing showers of spiritual blessing accompanying their ministry, there are but empty vaporings and idle

---

* The root of our word "clergy."

threatenings. In place, too, of divine certainty, because based on the Holy Scriptures, their fanciful theories and ever-changing notions manifest the fact that they themselves are carried about by every wind of human teaching, ever learning and never able to come to the knowledge of the truth.

They are further described as "autumnal trees without fruit, twice dead, rooted up." Having a fair outward appearance, they are like trees which in the season of fruit bear only leaves—like the fig-tree cursed by the Lord, which dried up from the roots. These indeed are "twice dead," for they are "dead in trespasses and sins," and dead too in a false profession, having a name that they live, but actually lifeless. "Every tree," said the Lord Jesus, "that my heavenly Father hath not planted shall be rooted up." So these are seen already, in God's estimation, as plucked up by the roots. In man's eye they make a fair show in the flesh, and tower skyward in loftiness and apparent beauty; but in the sight of Him who seeth not as man seeth, their judgment is already pronounced.

Impatient of restraint or rebuke of any kind, they are next likened to "raging waves of the sea, foaming out their own shame." It is not that they feel shame or remorse because of what they say or do ; but by their very speech they manifest the true condition of their lawless wills when confronted with the Word that exposes the hollowness of their contentions. "The unjust knoweth no shame;" but they proudly glory in what might well abase them before God and man. Blessed it is for those who seek to cleave to the Lord with purpose of heart, that He has set bounds to this sea, as to that in nature, beyond which its angry waters cannot go. He makes the wrath of man to praise Him, and the remainder of wrath He restrains. (See Ps. 76 : 10.)

The last awful figure portrays the doom yet awaiting these impious triflers in holy things. They are "wandering stars, to whom has been reserved the gloom of darkness for eternity." Like lost planets hurled out of their natural orbit, they flare brilliantly for the moment, then plunge off at a tangent into ever-deepening darkness as they rush through the fathomless depths of space farther and farther from the Source of light. Such shall be the end of all who now refuse the Light of life, and prefer instead to kindle their own fire, and compass themselves about with sparks (Isa. 50 : 11).

Solemnly the Holy Spirit says to every child of grace, "From such turn away" (2 Tim. 3 : 5).

ENOCH'S PROPHECY.

"And Enoch, the seventh from Adam, prophesied also as to
these, saying, Behold, the Lord has come amidst His holy
myriads, to execute judgment against all ; and to convict all the
ungodly of them of all their works of ungodliness, which they
have wrought ungodlily, and of all the hard [things] which ungodly sinners have spoken against Him" (vers. 14, 15).

THE source of Jude's information as to this
prophecy of "Enoch the seventh from Adam," is
not given. Criticism has busied itself to find out,
but all to little purpose, and certainly to no profit.
An apocryphal book of Enoch there is, which dates
evidently from pre-Christian times, and which contains language very similar to that here recorded,
but the nature of the book forbids the thought that
it, in any sense, is a part of, or can be placed on the
same plane as the Holy Scriptures; yet its use of
the words referred to makes it evident that in some
way, whether orally or in writing, God has seen fit
to preserve Enoch's prophecy, so that it was readily
incorporated into the weird book to which some
dreamer gave the name of the one who was translated that he should not see death. Jude, by divine
inspiration, declares the words were uttered by the
patriarch, and that they are to have their full application and final fulfilment, in common with all
prophecy, at the ushering in of the yet future day
of the Lord.

A partial fulfilment they had in the flood. A
more complete one awaits the appearing of the
Lord Jesus, in manifested glory, to take vengeance

on all who have refused His grace and done despite to the Holy Spirit.

What is referred to here is something very different to the happy event predicted in John 14 : 1–3 ; 1 Cor. 15 : 51, and 1 Thess. 4 : 13–18. In those scriptures, the theme is the return of the Lord to translate His saints to heaven, of which Enoch's rapture was a type. This may transpire ere the reader lays down this little book. In a moment, the Lord may descend and call all His own to meet Him in the air. But this will not be their, or His, manifestation before the world; that will take place later; the judgment-seat of Christ and the marriage-supper of the Lamb intervening above; while on earth apostasy will rise to its full height in the revelation and acceptance of Antichrist, and the utter rejection of all that is of God.

Then, when the cup of guilty Christendom's iniquity is full, the Lord shall come to the earth with myriads of His holy ones—redeemed men and unfallen angels—to execute the judgment long foretold upon the despisers of His word.

A very similar expression occurs in chap. 14 of Zechariah's prophecy : "The Lord my God shall come, and all the saints with Thee " (ver. 5). In each passage "saints" or "holy ones" does not, of itself, necessarily refer to redeemed humanity. Angels are also thus spoken of, and some would therefore limit the application to them alone. But Scripture clearly teaches the double aspect of the second coming of the Lord alluded to above. He is coming *for* His saints (John 14 : 3 ; 1 Thess. 4 :

15–17). He is also coming .*with* them (Col. 3 : 4). Caught up to meet Him as He descends with a shout, they will return with Him in manifested glory—when Enoch's prophecy and that of Zechariah shall be fulfilled.

Then will righteousness reign—every enemy being destroyed. No longer will impious deceivers profit by a profession of Christianity while secretly working to undermine the faith of God's elect, and turning the grace of God into lasciviousness. To every one will be rendered according to their works.

The present period (from the cross to the coming again of the Lord) is denominated by the Holy Spirit "man's day" (see 1 Cor. 4 : 3, marginal reading). While it lasts, God endures with much long-suffering vessels of wrath fitted, by their pertinacity in gainsaying His word, to destruction. But when man's day ends, the day of the Lord begins, when He who has been so long silent, while blasphemous and damnable heresies have been widely promulgated, to the ruin of untold myriads, will arise to act in judgment.

Then shall men who have despised the Word of Truth learn, when too late for blessing, that "all Scripture is given by inspiration of God."

Reader : challenge your heart I pray you *now* as to how you will stand *then !*

UNHOLY SEPARATISTS

"These are murmurers, complainers, walking after their own lusts; and their mouth speaks swelling words, admiring persons for the sake of profit. But ye, beloved, remember the words spoken before by the apostles of our Lord Jesus Christ, that they said to you, that at the end of the time there should be mockers, walking after their own lusts of ungodliness. These are they who set [themselves] apart, natural [men], not having the Spirit" (vers. 16–19).

JUST as the true servant of the Lord bears not only the doctrine of Christ, but commends himself by the manifestation of the fruits of the Spirit, so Satan's false apostles not only come with the sophistical denial of the truth upon their lips, but there are characteristic signs that soon make known to the godly the presence of these wolves in sheep's clothing. They may attempt to lisp in the voice of the believer, but their habits and ways betray them.

Like the mixed multitude who came up out of Egypt, in company with redeemed Israel, those of whom Jude writes to warn us are murmurers and complainers. Never having learned the initial lesson of subjection to God, they soon find the path of outward obedience to His word unspeakably irksome, for "the carnal mind is not subject to the law of God, neither indeed can be." Hence their continual objecting to the plainest precepts of the Holy Scriptures.

Aiming only to please themselves, they walk unblushingly after their own lusts, using their sacred calling as a ladder to worldly gain and ecclesiastical preferment. Self-denying service for Christ's sake, constrained by His all-conquering love, they understand not, yet resent with indignation the suggestion that greed for mammon and power is the actuating principle controlling them. But He who seeth not as man seeth has searched them through and through, and here records their true character as discerned by those Eyes which are as a flame of fire.

Great swelling words fall glibly from their uncircumcised lips as they boast of human progress and accomplishments, while forgetting the dreadful fact that man's will, until subdued by divine grace, is as much opposed to God as ever it was in the past— even when it nailed His blessed Son to a gibbet and poured contumely on His devoted head. Forgetting His sorrows, they pander to the ordered system of things that slew Him, and now fain would adorn His sepulchre.

The fifth count against these deceitful workers is one to which the majority are now so accustomed that it never occurs to them as one of the special signs of the apostasy—"Admiring persons for the sake of profit." The extent to which the public laudation of church dignitaries is often carried (even in their very presence) is shameful and disgusting.*

---

*At a recent meeting, where the writer was one of an audience of about three thousand persons, one D. D. introduced another Rev. Dr. as follows: "For years some of us have sat at the feet of this Gamaliel of the Occident, sometimes wondering, sometimes approving. sometimes venturing for the moment to disapprove, but ever carried at last by this master of men, this mighty brain-worker, to see the strength of his positions and to accede to his

Adulation is carried to such an extreme as to be positively nauseating ; but it is the order of the day, and will become increasingly marked as man is, inch by inch, pushed into the place of God and His Christ, till the full consummation of the Man of Sin of 2 Thess. 2. The deification of humanity and the humanizing of Deity in the minds of men is the natural outcome of all this. How different was the spirit of Elihu, who, having no advantage or profit of his own to seek, could speak with all due deference before the aged, yet with firmness declare, "Let me not, I pray you, accept any man's person, neither let me give flattering titles unto man. For I know not to give flattering titles ; in so doing my Maker would soon take me away" (Job 32 : 21, 22).

Well it is for the soul who seeks to be guided by Scripture to remember that nothing which he beholds on every side was unforeseen by God. Unbelief and apostasy may abound, but nothing takes Him by surprise. Long since, the apostles of the Lord Jesus Christ had warned us that the last days would be characteristically days of spiritual declension and departure from the truth. The coming of mockers, walking after their own unholy desires, has been foretold from the beginning.

---

views. Such an intellectual genius appears but seldom in a generation," etc., etc., *ad nauseam*. The Lord Jesus said, "How can ye believe which receive honor one of another, and seek not the honor that cometh from God only?" It should be added that both lecturer and chairman above referred to were pronounced "higher critics."

For the simple believer there is both strength and encouragement in this. If he look about him and see, as it were, star after star falling from heaven, teacher after teacher apostatizing from the truth, the love of many waxing cold, 'with error proudly defiant and apparently carrying all before it, he is apt to be overcome by fear and gloom. Like the prophet, he will be ready to cry, "Truth is fallen in the street, and equity cannot enter. Yea, truth faileth; and he that departeth from evil maketh himself a prey" (Isa. 59: 14, 15). But he may forget to add, with the same prophet, "The Lord saw it, and it displeased Him that there was no judgment." But let him remember that all that is so solemn in the on-rushing tide of evil has been foreknown and foretold long ago by Him who knows the end from the beginning, and he at once begins to take heart. He realizes that he is not to expect anything else. Therefore what he sees but the more firmly establishes him in the truth of Scripture. And, more than that, it is in the time of the end all this iniquity is to come to its height, before being forever overthrown by the personal appearing of the Living Word as King of kings and Lord of lords. Therefore he finds encouragement in the very darkness of the scene to expect soon to behold the shining-forth of the Morning Star, and later the rising in glory of the Sun of Righteousness.

This is the value of prophecy, which is as a light shining in a dark place, until the day dawn, and the daystar arise in the heart (2 Peter 1: 19). Led on by this sure and steady gleam, the humble child of God will not be dazzled by the pretensions, nor disheartened by the evil influence, of these haughty resisters of the truth, who set themselves apart as a select circle, who have attained to what the commonalty of Christians have not yet reached. There is a spiritual and carnal separation. The former is separation from evil at the call of the word of God, when to longer continue in some particular association would be unfaithfulness to Christ. The latter is a walking apart in fancied superiority, led on by pride and vainglory. This is what marks out the class Jude is portraying, *in the day of their power.*

For it should be noted that the apostle evidently traces for us the growth of the apostasy. He begins with evil workers privily creeping in, under cover of a Christian profession. Ere he closes they are pictured as having cast off all fear, as though their very strength made the necessity for it to have ceased. In place of caution and covered tracks, we have superciliousness and hauteur of the superlative degree, even to the forming among themselves of a select separated coterie, who arrogate to themselves all spiritual light and privilege, as well as human learning and scholarship.*

But great swelling words, even when coupled

. * Something of this is seen in the way in which critical rejectors of inspiration write and speak : "All scholars are now agreed that so-and-so is not true, or authoritative;" "No scholar now denies" this or that point for which they are contending. But the simple reader need not think such pretentious expressions have any real weight. Thousands of spiritually-minded scholars reject the so-called "results" of Higher Criticism *in toto.*

with the most arrogant presumption, can never overthrow the truth of the Eternal, nor alter the word, "The Scriptures cannot be broken."

Of the word of God, as of the Son of God, it can be said, "Whosoever shall fall on this stone shall be broken; but on whomsoever it shall fall, it shall grind him to powder." God is silent now, while men blaspheme His name and stumble over His word. Soon He will speak from heaven, when all shall know with whom they have to do !

Then it will be manifested that those who opposed Him, in their pride, were but natural, or soulish men, bereft of the Spirit. "The natural man receiveth not the things of the Spirit of God: for they are foolishness unto him: neither can he know them, because they are spiritually discerned" (1 Cor. 2: 14). This explains the difficulty many have in regard to believing the great truths of Scripture. They are unregenerate, natural men, attempting to act as ministers of Christ. But their speech betrayeth them.

Faith's Resource

"But ye, beloved, building up yourselves on your most holy faith, praying in the Holy Spirit, keep yourselves in the love of God, awaiting the mercy of our Lord Jesus Christ unto eternal life. And of some have compassion, making a difference; but others save with fear, snatching [them] out of the fire; hating even the garment spotted by the flesh" (vers. 20–23).

Dark and gloomy as the picture has been drawn for our warning by the pen of inspiration, there is yet no cause for despair. "Upon this rock," said Christ, "I will build my Church, and the gates of hades shall not prevail against it." The final result is sure. Victory will rest on the blood-stained banner of the Prince of Peace. In the hour of His triumph His faithful ones shall be the sharers of His glory. And in the present moment of their trial and His rejection they have an abundant solace and cheer, however the power of Satan may be manifested and error seem to be about to vanquish truth.

The saint of God needs to daily build himself up on his most holy faith. It is the revealed will of the Lord that is so called here, as in verse 3. That faith has been once for all revealed. On it the believer rests. Assured that it forms a foundation impregnable to every attack by men or demons, he is now to build himself up upon it. This implies continual feeding upon the Word, that the soul may be nourished and the spirit edified.

But linked up with this we have prayer in the Holy Spirit: not perfunctory saying of prayers, but spiritual communion with God, bringing to Him every need and every difficulty, assured that He waits in grace to meet the one and to dissolve the other.   Praying in the Holy Spirit can only result from a walk in the Spirit.   For if there be not self-judgment, prayer will be selfish.   We shall ask and receive not, because asking that our own lusts may be gratified.   But when Christ is before the soul, and the heart is finding its delight in Him, the Holy Spirit will Himself indite those petitions that God delights to grant.

A definite command follows: "Keep yourselves in the love of God."   Mark, it is not, " Keep God loving you."   Such a thought is opposed to that glorious revelation of Him whose nature is love. The Cross has told out to the full all that He is. Daily the believer is given to prove this loving-kindness.   Nor does the apostle exhort us to keep loving God.   The divine nature in every believer rises up in love to Him whose grace has saved him. "We love Him because He first loved us."

But here we are told to keep ourselves in the love of God.   It is as though I say to my child, "Keep in the sunshine."   The sun shines whether we enjoy it or not.   And so God's love abides unchanging.   But we need to keep in the conscious enjoyment of it.   Let nothing make the tried soul doubt that love.   Circumstances cannot alter it.   Difficulties cannot strain it, nor can our own failures.   The soul needs to rely upon it, and thus be borne in triumph above the conflict and the discouraging episodes incident to the life of faith.

Then we have a fourth exhortation, carrying the heart on to the coming of our Lord Jesus Christ. We are to await His mercy unto eternal life. We have eternal life now, by faith in Him who is Himself the life eternal. But we are going on to the scene where life shall reign, where everything will be suited to the life we already have communicated by the Spirit. This is at the end of the way; so the trusting soul looks up in hope and waits in patience for the return of the Lord.

The next verse tells us how to deal with bewildered souls, led astray by the wicked deceivers against whom we have been warned.

There is considerable manuscript variation here. In addition to the text given above, the following is suggestive: "And some convict, when contending; but others save with fear, snatching them out of the fire; hating even the garment spotted by the flesh." There is not much difference in the meaning of the exhortations. Either would direct that a godly discrimination be used in dealing with persons taken by error. A hard and fast rule for treating all alike is contrary to this verse, and to the tenor of all Scripture.

Undoubtedly souls have been driven more completely into evil systems by the rigor and harshness of well-meaning but unwise persons who so dreaded contamination with the error that they did not seek, in a godly way, to recover and clear the deceived one before refusing him their fellowship. 2 John 10 is decisive and simple as to a wilful teacher of what is opposed to the doctrine of Christ.

Such are to be shunned, and even refused a common greeting.

But other methods apply to dealing with their dupes, often entrapped through ignorance; though undoubtedly a perverse will has been at work or they would have been kept by divine power in the truth. Often what is needed is to deal with the perverted one as to his ways, rather than the teaching he has imbibed. When there is self-judgment the Paraclete can be depended on to do His blessed work of guiding into all truth.

Others need to be snatched from the fire; energetic effort made to warn and deliver ere the evil gets so firm a hold upon them that it will be too late to seek their blessing. But in every instance one needs to remember that unholy teaching is defiling and linked up with unholy living; so, care must be exercised lest, in seeking to aid another, one become himself besmirched by the evil influence, and be thus made unfit to help others because his own fellowship with God in the truth has become marred.

Truth is learned in the conscience; and only as one walks carefully and soberly before God is there security from error. Because Hymenæus and Alexander did not maintain a good conscience, they made shipwreck of the faith—as have untold thousands besides (1 Tim. 1: 18–20): this is the necessary result of enlightenment in divine things depending on the Holy Spirit's activity in taking the things of Christ and revealing them to His own. Where He is grieved by a careless demeanor and loose ways He no longer establishes the soul in the truth, but His activity is manifested in bringing home to the conscience the sin and failure that have dishonored the Lord. Therefore, if there would be growth in the knowledge of His Word, there must be a walk in the power of the Spirit ungrieved.

So, in seeking the recovery of those who have erred from the truth, this ministry to the conscience must not be lost sight of. Otherwise there may be ability to overthrow the reasonings of one astray, to meet all objections by direct Scripture, even to cause one to see that his position is biblically and logically untenable, while yet the state of his soul is as wretched as ever.

But when the deceived one is dealt with in the fear of God, in holy faithfulness, his restoration to communion will be the first step sought: then he will be in a state to appreciate the seriousness of the evil teaching in which he has been taken as in a net when he wandered out of the right way.

But in all this there needs ever to be godly concern lest one become himself defiled when seeking to recover another from defilement. This is what is especially emphasized in verse 23.

The Doxology

"But to Him that is able to keep you without stumbling, and to set [you] with exultation blameless before His glory, to the only God our Saviour, through Jesus Christ our Lord, [be] glory, majesty, might, and authority, from before the whole age, and now, and to all the ages. Amen." (Verses 24, 25.)

WHAT a pæan of holy exultation with which to close a letter which has drawn so dark a picture of the dangers besetting the path of the man of faith! God lives and reigns. His power is limitless. His grace is boundless. His glory and majesty shall to all eternity remain unsmirched by all the evil thoughts and ways of ungrateful and insensate men. It is for the Christian to pillow his head upon these blessed and soul-inspiring truths, and thus rise above all discouragement, and so go on in holy confidence to more than conquer!

"Unto Him that is able!"— This is what gives new strength to the wearied warrior. Weak and helpless in himself, he looks up in faith to One who is able. and thus out of weakness is made strong.

Let the difficulties of the path be what they may —however thickly strewn with gins and snares of Satanic device—God is able to keep the trusting soul without stumbling. David knew this when he sang, "Yea, though I walk through the vale of death's shadow, I will fear no evil : for Thou art with me " This is enough for faith in the darkest and most trying hour. I may not see a step before me, but He who is able sees the end from the beginning, and bids me confide in His love and wisdom, and thus implicitly trust myself to His guidance.

No believer would question the power of God to keep him five minutes without stumbling. But He who can keep for five minutes can keep for sixty; and He who can keep for an hour can keep for twenty-four; and He who can keep for one day can keep all the days if the eye and heart be fixed upon Himself. For this very purpose our Lord Jesus Christ has been "separated from sinners," with whom He once walked in grace, the undefiled and undefilable Man on earth. He prayed, "For their sakes I sanctify Myself [or, set Myself apart], that they also might be sanctified through the truth." Thus He became in heavenly glory the object for His people's hearts, that, daily living "looking off unto Jesus," they might be kept from stumbling.

And as He has all needed stores of grace for the pilgrim path, so the end is sure. He is able "to set you with exultation blameless before His glory." There shall be no failure here : God has predestinated every believer to be conformed to the image of His Son. To this end Christ, who loved the Church and gave Himself for it, is now engaged in its sanctification and daily cleansing by water-washing of the Word, that He might present it to Himself a glorious Church, not having spot or wrinkle, or any such thing. Then shall the Eve of the last Adam be manifested in the same glory with Himself; and all because God is able! Blessed heart - refreshing, and soul - uplifting truths are these!

In verse 25 the Authorized Version ascribes adoration and praise to "the only wise God our Saviour." The Revised Version, and all later translations, omit the word "wise," as unsupported by the better authorities. But granting it to be an interpolation made inadvertently, or otherwise, by some pious scribe, how it tells the effect that the transcribing of this epistle had on this unknown soul! Contemplating it, his heart was filled, and he cried in hallowed ecstasy, "This God is the only wise God." It is indeed "He that is perfect in wisdom" with whom we have to do, who will never call back His word. He is indeed the *only* God, for all others are but the imaginings of men's minds. Nor is it as the Judge he views Him, but with purged conscience worships before the mercy-seat as he owns Him as our Saviour-God; for He it was who so loved the world as to give His only-begotten Son that we might live through Him.

Thus all blessing flows down to us from the heart of God "through Jesus Christ our Lord," in whose peerless name we return our feeble praises, and through whom will be manifested that to our Saviour-God belong all glory, majesty, might and authority, from before the age-times, in the present (despite the jarring note of sin), and through all the ages to come, when the full results of the Cross will be displayed in "a new heaven and a new earth, wherein dwelleth righteousness."

For this Christ Jesus gave Himself when He died

to put away sin by the sacrifice of Himself. Thus He became the Lamb of God who beareth away the sin of the world. Not yet do we see this fully accomplished, for the trail of the serpent still mars God's fair creation ; but His eternal purpose is working out; and when all the ages of time have run their course, the last remains of sin will be banished to the lake of fire, and the sinless ages of eternity will have been ushered in. Then shall God be all and in all forevermore, and none dispute His authority or seek to detract from His glory again.

"Amen," swells up from every believer's breast, and faith looks on with blest anticipation to the accomplishment of all His good promise. This affirmative word is, in the succeeding book (the Revelation), used by the Son of God as one of His own names, or titles. " These things saith the Amen, the faithful and true witness, the beginning of the creation of God " (Rev. 3 : 14). He is, in His own character, the affirmation of all God's plans and ways. Through Him all shall end in perfection, and thus all glory, majesty and dominion be ascribed to the God of all grace while endless ages roll on to infinity. Amen and Amen!

H. A. I.